MW01243630

Wonderfully Ordinary

Thoughts on Faith, Relationships, and a Life of Fullness

Sean Gould

To my darling bride Lindsey and my beloved children Evelyn and Adeline. You have made life brighter, fuller, and more wonderful than I could ever dream. I love you with my whole heart.

TABLE OF CONTENTS

Introduction
Ring Like Gold

I remember stirring awake as a young kid to the sound of hymns reverberating from our 1970s Baldwin piano. I can see her silhouette swaying in the corner of the living room. My mom and the Baldwin illuminated from the light flooding through the drapes. Her music was the alarm clock ushering in the sunrise.

The piano smelled like old wood, felt, and metal. It would groan and roar beneath my mother's touch. If I close my eyes, I can still hear the notes, the sound of her pressing the pedal, and the hum of the strings. For as long as I can remember, I've had a deep appreciation for music, and I think my affection for it is rooted in those memories.

There are songs that seem to reach more deeply into your life than others. The type of song that can transport you to a specific moment in your life—as if a highlight reel were rolling as you listened. The song "Empire State of Mind" by Jay-Z was on the radio during my senior year of high school when I totaled my

2001 Honda Civic. When I listen to it now, I smell pavement and smoke. Anytime I listen to the song "Thing About Us" by Steve Moakler, I immediately imagine the first dance at my wedding. It recalls the breeze of early June, family and friends laughing around the banquet table, and the fiery glow of a Virginia sunset. Music has power over our lives.

Melody and harmony have an extraordinary way of speaking to our stories. It has the force to produce emotions and affections we could hardly touch otherwise. There's this riveting strength that lyricism has on us. Certain pieces of music put words to feelings we would have a hard time explaining otherwise. Music is seemingly magical, yet intensely relatable. There are ways that music can speak to you that no other form of art can.

One of my favorite folk records is called "The Stable Song" by Gregory Alan Isakov that he recorded alongside the Colorado Symphony. "The Stable Song" reminds me of summer holiday in college when I would sit on the back porch at sunset. It makes me experience the wonder of lightning bugs glowing in the fading sun, crickets chirping in the lower woods, and the scent of azalea, sumac, and rose. A thunderstorm would roll over the shadows of the Blue Ridge Mountains. Clouds would stretch across the sky, rain fell, wind howled, and then all fell silent as the stars and moon began their dance.

This Gregory Alan Isakov tune always awakens deep affections in my heart. For some reason, it tends to draw me into nostalgia, enchanting my head and heart with revelry for my life's story. "The Stable Song" is unhurried, warm, and rich with narrative. There's a verse toward the end of the song that always brings me to tears:

> And I ached for my heart like some tin man
> When it came oh it beat and it boiled and it rang
> Oh it's ringing
> Ring like crazy, ring like hell
> Turn me back into that wild-haired gale
> Ring like silver, ring like gold
> Turn these diamonds straight back into coal[1]

Ring like gold. This, to me, is the sound of a life of fullness. A heart that once was lost and lifeless but is now beating and ringing with purpose and significance. A life transformed. A heart alive to the God who created it.

Instead, what I had often experienced in my story was an ache for my heart like some tin man—feeling the hollowness of humanity east of Eden. My soul wasn't pulsing with purpose and felt unalive most of the time. What was I missing?

For years I felt the soulful tug between what I was experiencing in my daily life of faith and what I was observing in other people's stories. There was a disconnect between what was presented to me as the Christian life and what turned out to be a truly wonder-filled faith. For a long time, I viewed Christianity as a system of obligations and prohibitions.

Somewhere along the way I began to identify my relationship with Jesus strictly by Christian morality and ethics. And while I certainly believe sound doctrine and spiritual practice are essential to a life of faith, I've learned that it must be married with authentic, heartfelt experiences with God. When we view walking with Jesus as only rites and rituals, it becomes more of standing in place than a lovely life-giving adventure through the countryside. It is through an immersive, intentional, and intimate relationship with Jesus that we truly discover the heart of God. While theology may act as the bones our faith, union with Jesus is what brings breath and blood.

For years, my life felt clouded by religion and rules. Tiptoeing the lines. Climbing an endless ladder of self-justification. Never progressing in my character to the degree I expected. My hope to become the truest and best version of myself was marginalized by life's sorrows, disappointments, and uncertainties. Life felt dull. Christianity, so I thought at the time, had sold me a bill of goods.

Little did I know, a life of exuberant faith was waiting to be discovered not in the spirit of religion, but in the living Maker himself and his created world around us. *Wonderfully Ordinary* is my personal awakening and surrender to being loved by God. It is a collection of stories and encouragements for living a life with Jesus in an everyday world. A reflection on faith, memories, and realities pointing toward the gracious heart of God and his sincere longing for us. This is a mere spark amongst the fiery blaze by other heroes of the faith, compelling us to consider the wonderful workings of God in the commonplaces of our lives. It is a modest attempt encouraging the believer to drop the act, be the bundle of paradoxes you are, and discover true faith in a deeply personal relationship with God.

So, I'm writing, I suppose, hoping to move a few more steps in the direction of the resurrection dawn. Or at least (and I can only speak for myself) to stop trying to force things, relinquish control, and somehow receive the unending love of the Father. Believing Jesus when he so lovingly uttered,

> "Are you tired? Worn out? Burned out on religion? Come to me. Get away with me and you'll recover your life. I'll show you how to take a real rest. Walk with me and work with me— watch how I do it. Learn the unforced rhythms of grace. I won't lay anything heavy or ill-fitting on you. Keep company with me and you'll learn to live freely and lightly" (Matthew 11:28-30 MSG).

My name is Sean Gould. I'm tired, worn thin, and burned out on religion. How I got there, why I left there, and why I tend to go back is the story of my life. But that is not the whole story.

I'm Sean Gould, and I'm prone to make idols of things. I can have fits of anger and rage. I envy others, and I'm easily enticed by immodesty. I'm quick to judge others. I often find more satisfaction in the world than I do in the grace of God. I think about money more than I should, and I'm easily allured by food and drink that's not good for me. My life is a bundle of paradoxes. How I got there, why I left there, why I tend to go back, is the story of my life.

Yet, despite all of this, God is not repelled by me. Instead, he calls me his beloved. Wonderfully adored and completely redeemed. This is the larger and more important story, and only God in his incredible love knows the whole of it.

My longing is that through these pages you encounter the wonderful heart of Jesus, his heavenly workings within your story, and that your heart would awaken to the goodness of a wonderfully ordinary life. Where the magic of life is found in a deeply authentic relationship with Jesus. A story where adventure, wonder, and mystery are played out in our everyday lives. The sacred invitation to walk with God is all around us. And I hope we enter in.

Chapter One

Further Up and Further In

I used to think all extraordinary stories, the ones that had deep significance and made a difference in the world, were only lived by a certain type of person. These people often lived extravagantly, claimed fame for heroism, stood out in a crowd, or made a ton of money. As if there was this exclusive mold for living a life of fullness. An incredible story abounding with adventure and purpose. Growing up, I would lie awake at night wondering if my life would amount to anything. Life should be enchanting, I thought, but nothing in my story felt remotely close to magical. I kept questioning if I could live a life of wonder and purpose if my story wasn't filled with grand gestures or high profits.

I think of a story as an account of incidents and events in a person's life. It is a message and expression told through experiences and ordeals. A tale woven through the affairs and adventures of the story's character. Naturally, we are drawn to stories because they share information in a way that creates an emotional connection. This is why we get enraptured when we watch movies and read books. There's an individual in those adventures that desires something and overcomes conflict in order to get it. We connect and become captivated with the character as they develop through setbacks, disappointments, and triumphs. In essence, the story is evolving and forming alongside the character arch.

In every story, characters change and transform over the course of their personal journeys. For better or worse, the character's responses, actions, and decisions largely determine the trajectory of the narrative. In storytelling, the observer doesn't just get a glimpse of the character's temperament, but begins to relate, hate, or fall in love with the message being told. Fundamentally, a positive character arc is distinguished by some kind of victory or favorable growth, negative character arcs bend towards corruption or fall victim to flaws of their own personality, and the third arc is simply flat, where the character is categorized by no significant change.

Like a character in a movie or book, our personal lives are telling a greater story. We have our own character arc. We change, grow, and transform as we express to the world around us who we are based on our beliefs and actions. At the core, our life stories are rooted in our hearts. As we live out our stories, we're expressing to the people around us what lies at the very center of our personhood. If you want to know someone's true identity, their affections, and what they really desire, look at what they give their life to. Where we give our time, energy, and effort is ultimately an outward expression of an inward reality.

The Old and New Testament advocate for the human heart as the central animating center of all that we do. It is not just the command center of our emotions and affections but the place of origin for everything in our lives. It is the hub for who we are and where we operate from. Ultimately, the affections of our hearts determine the direction of our lives. This is why Jesus emphasizes that out of the abundance of the heart the mouth speaks (Luke 6:45), and its why Solomon expressed that above all else, guard your heart, for everything you do flows from it (Proverbs 4:23). The heart is the crux of humanity.

When my life wasn't telling much of an extraordinary story, I questioned my character arc. I wondered if the trajectory of who I was becoming was heading straight for a dead end marked by doubts and disappointments. My heart felt lost and led astray. I wasn't anyone special and didn't possess the attributes I imagined were needed for living a greater, more purposeful life. If there was a neon sign hanging in the window of my heart, it blinked and buzzed with words like "mediocre" and "ordinary."

I began to accept the notion that my story wasn't destined for a Hollywood ending since my life was far from a blockbuster hit. The ache in my heart was a symptom of things being fractured. Had I missed out on something? Was I told the wrong thing? Why did it seem like other people's stories had something I didn't?

If my life was rooted in my heart and not shaping up to be everything I had hoped, then ultimately my heart was placed in the wrong thing. There was some sort of fracture and disconnect in my core about what defined a fulfilling life. My confusion, doubts, and apprehension propelled me to search for answers. In a world of possibilities, I tested as many options and alternatives as I could.

I went looking for this wherever it was offered. I listened to the media, friends at school, the internet, and strangers. Unfulfillment made me exhaust all my options to make things right. I once heard relationships could bring a person a sense of completion. Maybe it was something the world convinced me to believe, but no matter how many friends I made or the number of dates I went on, I still felt unsatisfied. Success, achievement, and applause couldn't eliminate the emptiness either, it only masked it. Regardless of who I tried to become, there was always someone funnier than me, better-looking, more educated, or wealthier.

I tried the fake-it-until-you-make-it aphorism, which only suggested I had confidence, competence, and optimism. Meanwhile, I felt like a fraud while everything underneath the surface was completely rattled. I thought freedom and pleasure would offer some consolation and contentment, but those only left me more emptied of who I was. The moment I felt some sort of balance the scales would tip in the wrong direction. My life felt like a sandcastle being hit by a tsunami. At some point I considered that religion might offer a solution for what I was experiencing. Religious people at least looked like they had something figured out.

My family went to church growing up, but I never really cared for it. Most Sundays, I played hooky to get out of going, and the times I did go, I remember sitting on the floor in the bathroom to pass time. I'm not sure if it was the building or the bathroom, but there was always this stuffy aroma in the air. The white concrete walls felt constraining, and most of the people often came across as cynical and superficial. I don't mean to speak poorly of those people, but Christianity was making a lousy first impression. The life they were portraying didn't attract me to the God of the Bible.

How could something of antiquity truly transform my life here and now? My list of disappointments and concerns with Christianity and God only began to grow. The Christian life seemed to consist of an impossible set of laws to follow. The moral code was suppressive. Religion didn't seem like any better option for meaning, wonder, or purpose in life. God was dull and distanced.

The most thrilling time in my life growing up involving God was when I kissed a girl under the sanctuary pews of that same old church. It left me with a cocktail of emotion, excitement, and contempt. I remember the anxiety I felt wondering what people would say if they knew what I was doing, and I can still sense the fear that tightened in my chest as I considered what God thought about me.

It all felt like another dead end. My heart ached with emptiness even deeper than when I first set out with my questions of fulfillment. Any shot I had at discovering a thrilling and meaningful life had come up short. Every means that promised me vindication and satisfaction were only broken promises.

If the answer to the longing I felt deep within my soul was out there, I surely hadn't found it in this world. There was no way of getting my hands on it. I was utterly convinced that the only way my life would change at this point was through something transcendent. And that's the wild thing. Slowly and unwaveringly, heaven arose on me like the sun does in spring at the end of winter. The Sacred One came to me with warmth and affection shaking my bones and unraveling my heart.

I remember the first time I met Jesus. It was during my freshman year of high school when I was contending with all sorts of insecurities. He was in his early twenties, had recently graduated college, and every rumor you heard about him was different. I hadn't met him, so I didn't know what to believe besides gossip. Until one day when I was standing in the hallway after dismissal, and he walked straight towards me. Braces lined his teeth, and his hair was down to his shoulders. He wore faded blue jeans cuffed at the ankles and his leather sandals were worn on the soles.

He reached out his hand with optimism and genuine interest in his voice, "Hey man, my name is Cliff. It's good to meet you. What's your name?"

"Um, Sean. Yeah. My name is Sean…" I sputtered in a tone that suggested I had forgotten my name and never held a conversation with another human before.

"Right on, it's good to meet you, Sean." He could see I was struggling with what to say next, and said, "I'm not sure where you're heading, but I'm going to the student parking lot to say hello to a couple friends before they leave for the day. Do you want to join me?" His invitation was filled with such enthusiasm and sincerity that the only option I had was yes.

I tried making a quick joke about having to go to the weight room, but who was I kidding? I was a scrawny freshman that hadn't touched anything remotely heavy in my life. On the outside, it created space for me to seem like I had important alternatives to consider, but on the inside, I had already answered. Cliff had subtly gained my approval by stopping and showing that he cared to know me. He showed genuine interest in who I was just by looking me in the eyes, asking a few questions, and offering friendship.

There was authenticity in his voice that conveyed something was different about him. Cliff was headed somewhere. Not just to the parking lot, but somehow deeper in life. At the time, I didn't have words to describe it, but Cliff had something propelling him forward into his story. I knew wherever he was going I wanted to tag along. Whatever Cliff possessed that gave him this vigor for life might be exactly what I was searching for.

"Yeah, Cliff. I'm in," I said with curiosity and anticipation. Not knowing how that moment would change the trajectory of my life forever.

Cliff and I spent a lot of time together after that first interaction. It turned out that Cliff was a Young Life leader who spent most of his time with high school kids like me. Teenagers who were searching for life, often in all the wrong places. We logged some serious hours together playing sports, swimming in lakes, and hiking trails. There wasn't much ground in that mountain town we didn't tread together. We were constantly going places, making other friends, and discovering new things about life.

The drive he had for life was fueling mine and stirred my heart for adventure. It all traced back to when he asked me after dismissal that fateful day, "Do you want to come with me?" The same question he asked every time he would pull into the student parking lot in his silver Toyota 4Runner. It was an invitation into friendship, faith, and a life of fullness. Cliff became a genuine friend who cared deeply about the person I was becoming. He cared about my character arc. He cared about my story.

Time after time, he invited me into the story of his life where faith and wonder clashed head-on. We scaled the edge of mountains together, yet some of the most thrilling and life changing moments occurred when I was caught hanging on his words. You see, the way Cliff spoke about a person's life was unlike anything I had ever known. He talked about life like it told a story—a faithful and wildly incredible narrative. Words like "adventure," "joy," and "intention" were familiar to him, and he believed in them. Come to find out, everything Cliff ever talked about described a person he met and gave his life to years ago. A man named Jesus.

This man Jesus became vividly wonderful to me the more and more I learned about him. I soon found Jesus to be full of honesty, brilliance, and grace. Wildly different than anything anyone had ever portrayed to me. His kindness brought compassion and healing to broken people around him. I began to read these remarkable Bible stories and the miracles Jesus performed with new eyes. I studied the ways Jesus would treat people, restore broken families, heal the sick, and bring redemption to the outcast. Jesus, who I had only ever experienced as a distorted blur from afar, drew near to me so I could see him clear as day. This man, Jesus, was for people. He was for me. His heart beating and pulsing to welcome people into a right relationship with him.

John Eldredge writes in Beautiful Outlaw that Jesus is, "the playfulness of creation, scandal and utter goodness, the generosity of the ocean and the ferocity of a thunderstorm; he is cunning as a snake and gentle as a whisper; the gladness of sunshine and the humility of a thirty-mile walk by foot on a dirt road."[1] He is all those things and wonderfully more. As the religious fog began to fade from my eyes, the relational invitation to engage the God of the universe through Jesus became clearer and brighter. As the Apostle Paul said, everything is created, held together, and reconciled in Jesus:

> Christ is the visible image of the invisible God. He existed before anything was created and is supreme over all creation, for through him God created everything in the heavenly realms and on earth. He made the things we can see and the things we can't see—such as thrones, kingdoms, rulers, and authorities in the unseen world. Everything was created through him and for him. He existed before anything else, and he holds all

creation together. Christ is also the head of the church, which is his body. He is the beginning, supreme over all who rise from the dead. So he is first in everything. For God in all his fullness was pleased to live in Christ, and through him God reconciled everything to himself. He made peace with everything in heaven and on earth by means of Christ's blood on the cross.

(Colossians 1:15-20 NLT)

This Jesus is utter goodness—the most human of humanity with the heart and mind of God. Everything about Jesus is everything I had longed for yet didn't know existed. The depths of my soul longed for the life Jesus promised. Not a broken thing like all those other idols teased. All I had ever known in my life up to this point was hollow and disappointing, but Jesus offered meaning and significance. Those long restless nights of anxiety and worry collided with the Prince of Peace. I was created for something greater and had discovered it in a person.

Jesus, embodied in the life of Cliff, hit the bullseye of my unbelieving and lonely heart. I began to see the adventure of faith as having a relationship with the creator of the universe as many of my misconceptions of God started to fade away in the goodness of Jesus. I learned I didn't have to be put together or have everything figured out. I realized I could be a bundle of paradoxes and loved all the same. Cliff was simply inviting me into something he had already discovered himself. A life marked by a relationship with Jesus. An incredible life telling an even greater story about God and his ferocious heart for you and me.

I used to believe all extraordinary life stories, the ones that seemed to carry weight and mean something, were only lived by people who had the most remarkable resumes. Resumes made up of power, possessions, and prestige. Now I realize the most significant life narratives are created through people who have found true fulfillment in Jesus. Receiving the terrifying and wonderful things of life as an opportunity to transform and flourish. Where life is not about accumulating applause, wealth, or respect, but instead rooted in the adventure of faith played out in our everyday world. A deeply rich life transformed and made anew by the love of God. A story that speaks of grace for the broken and contrite.

As I read the Bible now, it's much more of a treasure map guiding me through this untamed tale of life. It's an instrument pushing and pulling on my heart that ultimately points homeward towards the creator. It's a roadmap to navigate the roads of faith, doubt, and blessing in life. It drives me further into becoming the person God made me to be. A way to discover more of him and his heart for humanity.

I find a lot of comfort reading about people in the Bible meeting Jesus for the first time. Jesus so often says what Cliff said to me when I first met him: "Come follow me." It's the right way to live your life really—inviting others into God's story because you've tasted and seen the goodness for yourself. A story you've come to cherish so much that you can't keep it to yourself.

Donald Miller wrote in Blue Like Jazz that, "Sometimes you have to watch somebody love something before you can love it yourself. It is as if they are showing you the way."[2] I think this sentiment reflects the Christian faith. I've come to know and love Jesus on a deeper level by witnessing other people encounter him for themselves. The orbit of faith is about orienting one's life around the heart of the Great Rabbi. The people who have been caught in God's gravity are those who step into ordinary moments and live with extraordinary love.

I've bumped shoulders with plenty of people in this world, but only a handful really live out their everyday stories with faith, playfulness, and courage. Individuals who don't leave their faith on the doorstep but carry it into their wonderfully ordinary lives. These are the types of people who step into the monotony of humanity with love and kindness.

They don't fast-forward through the disappointing and dreadful moments of life but instead look at those events as a channel for stronger trust. These folks have been compelled by God's love to live with deep intention, looking for the ways Jesus gives purpose in their daily lives. Tish Warren wrote in her book Liturgy of the Ordinary that, "...it's in the dailiness of the Christian faith—the making the bed, the doing the dishes, the praying for our enemies, the reading the Bible, the quiet, the small—that God's transformation takes root and grows."[3]

I believe the people who pursue Jesus in the simple day-to-day moments of life are the people who most often have deeper, more meaningful stories. These individuals are discovering the wonder of life by communing with an extraordinary God on an everyday level. It's connecting with God in the cycles of life. It's finding God while grieving over lost loved ones. Rejoicing in the miracle of newborn babies. Crying over broken friendships and relationships. Celebrating new chapters. Enjoying laughter and dinner parties. Tearing up over good strawberry ice cream on a summer evening. Staring in awe at sugar maples turning to colors of honey and merlot under an autumn sky.

These folks are the ones worth following and emulating. They are the people with stories worth listening to. Incredible lives telling an even greater narrative, the story of God and his abounding love for humanity. Stories about people who found life when they gave theirs away. For me, it took a committed person showing up in my life to model the real heart of Jesus.

Wonderfully Ordinary is a series of reflections and stories about people in my life who have pulled back the curtain on the remarkable story of God. It is a collection of encouragements for living a vibrant life with Jesus in an everyday world. And the open invitation for everyone to do the same.

This invitation welcomes us into the greatest narrative ever lived. One full of faith, wonder, and adventure pointing towards the gracious heart of God. It is a humble request encouraging the believer to drop the act, be the bundle of paradoxes you are, and discover authentic faith in a deeply personal relationship with Jesus. In the enchanting words of C.S. Lewis, I want to invite you along, "Come further up, come further in!"[4]

Chapter Two

Fences

My life, like many others, has been marked by humble beginnings. I grew up in Roanoke, Virginia, a quaint town nestled in the foothills of the Blue Ridge Mountains. It was the wild west of my youth. The setting for many firsts in my life. A lot of who I am today has been influenced by friendships, events, and experiences from there. I've come to appreciate my hometown much more since I moved away. It's almost as though I needed to leave in order to realize how much I really loved the place. Sometimes you have to let go of something so you can find it again. Let it reawaken a deeper and more vibrant affection in you.

Roanoke became the backdrop of my story well before I was born. My parents got married there, years beforehand, at the same church where I ended up making out with the girl beneath the pews. They eventually set their roots down in a small house on the outskirts of town and started to raise a family. Believe it or not, they still live in the same house all these years later.

My father is an innovator and dreamer. He's invented and brought countless products to market over the course of his wonderful life. Some ended up in bigger box stores and others never even reached the shelves. I imagine Theodore Roosevelt had a man like my dad in mind when he penned The Man in the Arena, writing that "The credit belongs to the man...who does actually strive to do the deeds; who knows great enthusiasms, the great devotions; who spends himself in a worthy cause; who at the best knows in the end the triumph of high achievement, and who at the worst, if he fails, at least fails while daring greatly."[1]

This poem is a great summation of who I believe my father to be. Who from a worldly perspective might have never made a big splash, but to those closest to him, know he's enjoyed the richness from the deeper things of life. Like a vibrant life-long marriage, strong relationships with his children, a heart for God, and a desire for peace. He's a lover and defender whose affections have always been for his bride and family.

My mom has a heart of gold. She's always been a steady fountain of courage and strength in our household. Her spirit is one of bravery and devotion even in the most difficult of times. She's the type of person to hope beyond hope, which buoyed the hearts of our family during some rough years. God's recipe when making Mary was a dash of sass, a pinch of spunk, and a whole lot of joy. She's the one who sang hymns of God's goodness over me as a little kid bruised by the world. My sister and I have lived in the wake of our parent's love and faithfulness to one another over the years.

They ran an ice cream cafe for most of my childhood. A mom-and-pop shop that demanded a lot of them. The restaurant business was hard and never really paid well. When sales were low, they found other odd jobs to make more money. We ate on free and reduced lunches at school. I'm not sure how they kept food on the table and clothes on our backs at times, but we never seemed to lack anything. We may have lived a modest life, but we reveled in the things that truly matter—love, kindness, attention, and affirmation.

Craig and Mary have always had blue-shaded collars, but their hearts are more colorful with hope and humility than the cotton-candied sky of a California sunset. I recognize now all the ways they sacrificed and gave their lives for us. I was grateful as a kid for their affectionate involvement in our lives, but I wrestled hard with our economic lowliness. Not to mention what it did to my heart at times over the years.

I believe we were all created with a deep desire for love and acceptance. It doesn't matter what your age, race, gender, political leaning, or religious affiliation might be, we all long for attention and affirmation. We live in a world in which approval and recognition reign supreme. We're constantly looking to things outside of ourselves for acceptance. This pursuit drives us to comparison, which often leads to discontentment.

Hollister-brand blue jeans were quite trendy when I was in high school. The kind that had paint splattered on the front, holes in the material, and worn-out seams. They're foolishly expensive considering how destroyed they are, but so many of my friends wore them at the time. However, I couldn't afford them, which led my easily influenced teenage self into a downward spiral of embarrassment. I wanted so badly to fit in and have the approval of my peers. To be liked because of a stupid pair of jeans. My friends had what I didn't. Comparison fueled resentment to bubble up in me.

I had qualms with the status of my family and what we couldn't afford. My heart boiled with frustration and hate for the hand I was dealt. I loathed my lot in life, and I'd have done anything to change it. As a silly teenager, I believed the lie that owning a certain brand of jeans would make me happy. I really believed possessing a specific product would make a difference in my life. As if those blue jeans had the power to bring a strange sense of fulfillment.

One day, I had the playful idea to take the bottom shelf pants I owned and alter them to look like the Hollister ones. I ran down to our basement workshop and began to alter them, hoping no one would notice the difference. I grabbed a can of wall paint and splashed some on the fabric. I snatched a piece of sandpaper from a drawer and began creating worn looking patterns on them. I even rummaged through one of my mom's old drawers to find a needle and thread for stitching together some of the holes I created. I worked on those jeans for countless hours trying to make them look like the Hollister brand. If I couldn't afford the real thing, I would compromise to have the fake version.

I was propelled by envy, and soon enough, had a product I was proud of. The only way someone would be able to tell the difference was by looking at the inside tag. I was completely wrapped up with approval and wanted its hollow sense of value. Soon enough, seasons changed, and those knock-off jeans were of no use to me anymore. The sense of contentment I found in those jeans was fleeting like winter changing into springtime.

It's obvious to look back on now, but I was insanely foolish to think those pants would bring my life any sort of fulfillment. Yet isn't this how we live our lives every day? Whether we admit it or not, we live with a false sense of what is going to bring us lasting fulfillment. We encounter discontentment in our lives as we look for satisfaction where it can't be found. If life is marked by where we look for wholeness of heart, then we are searching in all the wrong places.

I've noticed that most people around me these days never seem to be satisfied with their own lives. The grass is always greener on the other side of the fence. Every ad, show, movie, product, app, and trend suggest that new flings, new relationships, jobs, cities, food and drink, friendships, trips, or sex will satisfy the insatiable longing in our hearts. We constantly live our lives saying to ourselves, "If I had that thing, my life would be better."

This slippery slope leads us towards envy, jealousy, and comparison. It slowly convinces us that what exists over the fence will quench our lives. If I can be misled into thinking a pair of pants would do this, why would I think larger, more significant matters would be any different?

Another phrase often attributed to Theodore Roosevelt expresses what I refer to as the fence-effect when he expressed,

"Comparison is the thief of joy."[2] We throw around this proverb lightly without really understanding the gravity it bears in our lives. This message of comparison comes from a person who must have wrestled with the havoc it brings. I can only imagine someone like Roosevelt easily comparing himself to other presidents, world leaders, fathers, or public figures. It's been a hundred years since he coined the phrase that still reflects our world today.

We question our lives because our neighbors have the more expensive car or the nicer house. We complain about our careers because our colleague received the promotion, we've been working for years to achieve. We justify ourselves against strangers because they don't live with the same morality. We chase after other relationships because the infatuation has worn off in our current one. Our hearts bend heavily away from peace and contentment with our current lives as we compare ourselves to everything around us.

The good news for us is that the hope and power of the gospel of Jesus can silence comparison in our lives. It can mute the contrasting and allow joy to finally rule and reign. Until we allow the joy of the Lord to have its wholesome place in our lives, we will constantly wrestle with deep, heart-level dismay. We will finally begin to experience holy contentment when we surrender to the plans, purpose, and guidance of God in our lives.

The truth is, most often, the other side of the fence isn't nearly as green as we thought. The so-called greener side turns out to have its flaws and disappointments like anything else. The truth is, there really isn't a greener side, but unfortunately, we haven't stopped jumping fences for the so-called better life. A process that causes pain, heartache, and confusion to everyone in its wake. We go looking for a life we were never intended to live. Throwing our stories away as if there's something better out there. This type of living has no roots in God's design and intent for our stories.

The creation story establishes our identity and adequacy in God. We are fearfully and wonderfully created in his image. Therefore, our stories are given and sustained by God's divine will. Our entire lives are fearfully and wonderfully laid before us to be received with joy and contentment. They are not intended for us to take lightly and wish away. God desires for us to uncover his specific purposes for our lives here and now. Yet, we constantly want to alter ours or trade them in for something else altogether.

Our fleshly tendencies cause us to doubt God in frustration and disappointment. We're convinced we know what's better for our lives. We grab hold of another fence, another option, another worldly promise, and we jump for it. This idea creeps into life at the dawn of time in the Garden of Eden.

Adam and Eve were discontent and deceived. They wanted life to be different. They wanted to be like God. The fruit from the tree of the knowledge of good and evil looked pleasing and desirable but was terribly not so. They reached and ate out of their own wisdom. The result was absolutely devastating.

When we live out our stories through any perspective other than God's, we lose sight of our belovedness, identity, and worth. We begin to resent our lives, relationships, friendships, and community. We compromise and turn to counterfeit items. We burn out and point fingers at God, believing we've been shorthanded. We find ourselves slaving over a pair of jeans in a basement, hoping to find lasting contentment where it can't be fulfilled.

It's in those moments of doubt when we need to remember who we are in God. There is much healing needed when we've strayed so far from home. It is in those lost moments when we need our bent perspectives to be made new. We need to find our true lives in God again. It is the process of coming back home. It is resting in the arms of the Father.

Aligning with God is re-centering our stories on the truth that we've been given all it takes to live a life of godliness right where we're planted regardless of circumstances. We are exactly where God wants us. And if not, his Spirit will move us in the right direction. We need to trust that God's heart towards us is good, especially in those everyday moments of life when the fence looks so tempting.

We need to hold onto God's promises in those menial days when we're exhausted from changing diapers or we've cried our eyes out because we'd love to have a baby to care for, but infertility has left its mark. We need to cling to the Gospel's assurance in those moments when we get the call with a terrifying diagnosis. Especially in the times when we don't feel like our lives measure up. In the monotony of loading the dishwasher, doing laundry, or taking out the trash.

We need to cling to the life that Jesus offers us. A story and promise of good purpose, not good fortune. Where Jesus guarantees he will shepherd us. Where we have no need for those other unfulfilling devices. The life we've been searching for is right under our noses, not in some far-off fantasy land or over some fence. It does not exist in the bigger house down the street, in a brand-new car from the dealership, a night out on the town, or in that big promotion.

While all those things are fine in themselves, heaven wants to make itself most known in your personal heart. We should not wish away our current circumstances, but rather ask ourselves what God has in store for us right here and now. On your side, in your life, and in your story.

There are visions and hopes we have for our stories. We have natural desires we hope come true. Some do, and others don't. Jesus delights very much in our hearts and what flows from them. He delights in our stories because he is shaping and shifting them to align with heaven. The frontier of our stories is a lovely, yet wild place. We must keep our eyes on Jesus, the author and captain of our faith. He will hold and press us in the direction we need to go. The closer we get to him, the more we'll discover the purposes he has for our lives.

God is working within our hearts to show us we have all we need in him. There are diamonds on your side of the fence. Treasure and riches hidden in your life waiting to be unearthed. Take time to dig deeper where you are. Look at the life right before your eyes and pay attention to where Jesus is already at work. Pray for your eyes to be opened to the wonders of God here and now. Seeking Jesus in our daily lives is a beautiful process of discovery. It doesn't have to be in some extraordinary way, but deeply over time.

I'm not always able to look back and understand God's work in my life over the years, but I can tell you while I was altering a pair of jeans, he was there. In my shallow comparison, God was trying to show me I had all I needed in him. Our lives have adequacy because Jesus has said so. He is the one who brings fulfillment and contentment into the wonderfully ordinary moments of our lives. Stop comparing your story to others. Take hold of your life and discover what Jesus wants to do with it. I can promise you he is waiting to reveal his heart and kingdom to you right where you are.

Chapter Three

Eugene

I've always admired people who cultivate purpose and resilience in their life stories. Where the narrative they're writing with their lives is rooted in faithfulness and intention. I often wonder how these people become so grounded. Uniting the sacred with the ordinary. How do people become sturdy and steadfast through all of life's ups and downs? Why do these folks seem to thrive more than others? There must be some sort of recipe for human flourishing.

I'm describing people with marriages that don't just have the image of being lively but are truly vibrant and enduring. I'm referring to the person who is content in their everyday job and uses it to better their communities. It's the type of individual that cultivates depth and authenticity in their family life. The sort of person who seems to handle the ebb and flow of life's goodness and cruelty with the same boldness and courage.

These are just a few examples, but I think it's rare for someone's story to be filled with this level of intentionality and depth. I used to think there was a secret to cultivating a life beyond measure. A story where faithfulness, courage, and gentleness are some of the primary reflexes. Now I think it's just normal people embracing everything in life as sacred and deciding to make something deep and wonderful with it.

My grandfather, Eugene, was everything and more to me growing up. His hands were rough and calloused from years of being a carpenter, but they were always soft and inviting to pick me up when I would burst through the door as a young boy. His silvery hair was peppered by age, and the shape of the creases around his mouth showed he had a history of smiling. He smelled like pine and earth in the sort of way that makes you want to take a walk in the woods. His laugh rolled over you like a hearth fire crackling with warmth on a cold winter night.

Eugene was an incredibly talented carpenter. He built the whole house that my mother was raised in as a kid. It took him several long and exhausting years to finish the construction, but it turned out wonderfully. His entire family would enjoy their handcrafted home for many years to come. After my mom grew up and moved out to marry my dad, they ended up buying a house just up the street from my grandparents. Naturally, we spent a lot of time with them being so close.

I didn't get the privilege to see Eugene craft his art of carpentry in real time because most of his projects were done before I was born. Although he was primarily a carpenter, I remember him more as a gardener. Most days after school and on the weekends, we would head down to his house. Our car would pull down the long, dusty gravel drive lined with maples and pine. I would hop out of the back seat, shoot across the yard, and head straight into his garden. Eugene could always be found out there in his white t-shirt, blue jeans, and a cold glass of tea in his hand.

His garden was sprouting with vegetation and growth. I would lose myself between the rows of corn stalks as they towered over my head, my hands brushing their sides as I mazed about. The field was covered with tomatoes, lettuce, potatoes, carrots, and peppers. He nurtured apple and cherry trees that lined the garden and stretched along a bubbling creek. He pruned grape vines hanging from a trellis on the southside of the water. The smell of his beehives and honey lined the hillside. Everything seemed to flourish and propagate under Eugene's influence.

The garden was evidence of his toil and exertion over the years. It was the fruit of countless hours of laboring in the soil. A place once barren with dirt had become a space budding with harvest. Eugene's own little Eden blossomed in the hollow by the hill. All because he had a vision to see things flourish. This vision, paired with years of faithful work, cultivated a fruitful garden our family tasted and enjoyed.

A lot of conversations I've had recently make me think of Eugene's garden. Not because they're centered around horticulture but because they remind me that our lives are like gardens. In the same way gardens don't just grow overnight, I can't expect a fruitful and faithful life to just happen haphazardly. A harvest isn't reaped overnight. It takes countless hours of labor, science, and art to grow a vibrant garden.

The fruit of a well-crafted life is created through years of faithfulness. I've also heard it described as long obedience in the same direction. It's inward devotion, spurring you in an outward direction, that you stick with your whole life. Our lives, like gardens, are nourished and bloom to whatever level we invest in it. Like any blooming bed of flowers, our lives need the right care and attention to flourish.

We don't need to study gardening to grasp the basic science of growing plants. Anyone with a basic understanding of our ecosystem can tell you a garden is going to grow when a seed has been planted in good soil, where plenty of sunlight is available, the climate is suitable, and it is watered frequently. If all those components are working together in the garden, vegetation will grow. When we cast this same idea over our lives, we too will see that we need the right elements to flourish.

Human flourishing is experiencing the full extent of God's love and wonder in everyday life. From sustaining deep friendship and having a healthy relationship with work, to remaining steadfast when life is cruel. Flourishing is the heavenly fulfillment of God's good purposes in our stories. It is the everyday reality of a heart coming alive to the God who created it.

God has designed each of us to come alive and experience his love—unique ways for us to refocus on what God wants to do with our stories. Recognizing those habits will help us bring our attention back to the sacredness of life. If your heart is reminded of God's love for you by hiking in the mountains, find time there to gain rest for your soul. If you feel God's presence near rivers, create opportunities to get away there to recharge and reconnect. Maybe experiencing God's love looks like going on a run, making a tasty meal, enjoying an afternoon in the park, riding your bike, or sitting on your porch.

Sometimes refocusing the soul is simply pausing in solitude to remind ourselves of our belovedness and the sacred work God is doing around us. Whatever it may be, our souls need to be cared for before we can cultivate a better life. Our lives are only as vibrant and deep as our connection with God.

Relationships, vocations, neighborhoods, and households flourish based on their union to Jesus. What we plant in our lives will be what we harvest in our stories. Also, where we plant our lives will determine the depth of our stories.

The people I consider my heroes are those who have shaped their lives into something of beauty and deepness. They root themselves in the higher things. They live out their days with intention, considering all things as heavenly and worth being cultivated.

Everyone has the same amount of time each day to nurture what we can. Stewarding our stories in the mundane is central to cultivating an abundant life. We need to discover what elements nourish the soil of our souls.

Scripture often uses gardening and agriculture to illustrate the Kingdom of Heaven and its outpouring here on earth. For one, Jesus uses a vineyard to describe the life-giving union between God and man when he explained:

I am the true vine, and my Father is the gardener. He cuts off every branch in me that bears no fruit, while every branch that does bear fruit he prunes so that it will be even more fruitful. You are already clean because of the word I have spoken to you. Remain in me, as I also remain in you. No branch can bear fruit by itself; it must remain in the vine. Neither can you bear fruit unless you remain in me. I am the vine; you are the branches. If you remain in me and I in you, you will bear much fruit; apart from me you can do nothing. If you do not remain in me, you are like a branch that is thrown away and withers; such branches are picked up, thrown into the fire and burned.

(John 15:1-6 NIV)

Jesus longs for our lives to flourish through abiding in his love. Resilience and fruitfulness come through remaining united to the true vine. The way towards cultivating purpose and resilience in our life stories is through union with the Father. Where we are rooted in the life source. Uniting the sacred with the ordinary.

The way a follower of Jesus becomes grounded in life is by connecting themselves to the wellspring that undoubtedly leads to flourishing. Becoming steadfast through the highs and lows of life is directly correlated to our union with Jesus. This is why some folks seem to thrive more than others. The recipe for human flourishing is rooted right there in the Book of John.

Let's not brush past the vineyard illustration either when Jesus depicts our need for pruning. There are also plenty of things we need removed from our lives for growth to happen. Things that are distracting and disruptive. The lives we are capable of living can only be experienced through pruning.

Jesus is eager to make something radiant in us, but we've got to be willing for things to wither away for new things to thrive. True healing and restoration come in the deep recesses of our souls when we let the light in. Resurrection occurs after death. Habits, practices, and patterns will need to die for better, more heavenly things to grow in our lives. We may even experience barrenness at times, but the Lord promises to restore even this.

One of the biggest distractions from enjoying our union with God is by wanting the fruit more than the giver itself. We want the finished product without having to do the work with God to get there. We have an idea of how we hope things turn out, but we want it instantly.

We want to swim in the deep waters of a thriving marriage, raise a family to walk with Jesus, care for our surrounding community, experience justice and peace, and reach a content place in our vocations where we get to serve God and people. Unfortunately, we get frustrated with the process of pruning and sanctification because it's filled with setbacks and cul-de-sacs.

We may also find some wounds in us that have been kept covered over time. Maybe someone made a comment about your body, fracturing your self-image for years. Perhaps your partner cheated on you, and you've had difficulty trusting anyone since. Maybe you've been sober for years from an addiction, but there's still that trace of vice that bubbles up in you. Shame and sorrow have a sly way of distorting who we are. As we unearth the brokenness in our hearts, the love of Jesus will restore and return to us our true humanity and union with him.

I was never fond of addressing those buried, wounded parts of my personhood because it was uncomfortable, but now I realize it's a channel of God's grace. I often wonder if the resistance of our stories is the force that propels us into a heavenly life. As if the pressure and pain we feel is a bowstring ready to launch our lives into the love and purposes of God. Wishing away the tension may limit our ability to experience union with God and what he has planned for our stories.

The garden of our lives will never become what they can if we avoid the harsh and difficult stuff of life. Go unite with Jesus in the places of doubt, loss, and confusion of your heart. Let's remember that Mary Magdalene returned to the tomb aching with sadness after Jesus was crucified and found him but mistook him as a gardener (John 20:15).

Despite Mary's grief and woundedness, she returns to Jesus to find comfort and consolation. Though she faces terrible pain, and her vision is blurred by tears, she encounters the great gardener cloaked in wonder and love. Jesus so gently calls Mary by name and restores what she's lost. Jesus, mistaken through tears as a gardener. Let this encourage us to also bring our tears and pain to him for healing.

God, the great gardener of our souls, understands the long-term purpose and end of our stories. It makes sense that he would know the road to get there. Our lives need to be cultivated, shaped, and pruned in order to bear the fruits of the spirit (love, joy, peace, patience, kindness, goodness, faithfulness, gentleness, and self-control as mentioned in Galatians 5:22-23).

We must be united with Jesus to experience and enjoy the wholeness he offers. Tending our stories like gardens is central to cultivating an abundant and resilient life. The way we abide in Jesus now will shape who we become in our lives. As we remain connected to the vine, we unite the sacred with the ordinary. Union with Jesus is the full expression of our wonderful humanity. The very intent of our existence. We have all we need in Jesus to cultivate a faithful life.

Chapter Four

The Castle on The Hill

I realized I loved my hometown several years after I moved away. Roanoke is a beautiful Virginia town rooted in the Blue Ridge Mountains with its own definition of hustle and bustle, quaint country stores, and southern charm. As a kid, my childlike wonder would launch me into the great outdoors. I'd hike parts of the Appalachian trail in springtime as wild redbud and lilies bloomed in the countryside.

Summers were spent down by the riverbed off Back Creek fishing for bluegill and swimming the fresh water until the sun descended and the fireflies began to glow. I would lose track of time in the woods off Bandy Road, swinging from vines and hiding out in Eugene's tree house while the recurring summer storm would rumble over the lower hills and turn the sky azure and gray. Life as a young kid was filled with discovery and exploration.

Yet over time, I grew to resent it for being slow and dull. My love for it had waned. It became too small and sleepy for me. I used to think it was a place holding me back from experiencing the wide-open world. Something in me itched to move on.

I wonder if we all feel that way at times. As though we're trapped in our hometown, and if we don't escape, we'll never make it out. I used to think I was too good for Roanoke, and it was just a launching point into bigger and better things.

However, after many years removed, I've come to realize Roanoke offered more to me than I ever gave it in return. Donald Miller captures this idea in his adventure tale Through Painted Deserts when he penned, "Everybody has to leave, everybody has to leave their home and come back so they can love it again for all new reasons."[1]

This was true for me. I had to leave my home in order to love it again. I had to get away in order to really look back and understand the beauty and wonder that existed during my life at that time. I think there's more to this idea of home than we give credit to because I've come to find out that home is more than just a location on the map.

After all these years, I've come to realize that home doesn't necessarily have an address but an identity. Home is your people. Home is the compounding expression of community, family, and relationships in our lives. Life is built amongst the people cultivating that wonderful expression of home. For me, this experience of home has its beginnings in the longest relationship I know in my life outside of my parents. The amazingly vibrant friendship between my sister and me.

I honestly couldn't tell you what my first interaction with Lauren was like. What human being really remembers those first days outside the womb? I like to think my two-year-old sister at the time was absolutely enamored by her little brother and filled with excitement for all the ways we'd experience life together, but I'm sure it was more puzzling than anything else. I was brought into our family and welcomed into the world alongside Lauren. She was, and remains to this day, full of goodness, grace, and beauty. We grew up and experienced life together, and with that comes a bond and magic only siblings know.

Lauren was one of my very first experiences of home. She was the one to get me into trouble and the one to get me out. She took the brunt of my young fury and dealt her own in return. The sublime brother and sister rivalry grew deep. She was the first person I ever called my friend. The one I looked up to and went to about life questions. Lauren referred to our house as the castle on the hill. It was a quaint ranch-style home on the outskirts of town, but in our imaginations, it was our fortress.

We'd dance, play, and adventure around every inch of that house. We would tell one another stories, share emotions, and grow up together. She gave me love, encouragement, and care. The fondest emotions that only a sibling can evoke. Lauren had the charisma and character to make you believe in yourself; she still does. Her heart for me was the perfect invitation into a life overflowing with joy and wonder. She offered the ultimate recipe for home.

We experienced so much of life together that lingers with me still today. The origins of my family and Lauren's impact on my life remain weighty even now. If home truly is defined by the people we spend our time with, Lauren was the epitome of home. The compounding impression of many years and memories together formed a bond that provided safety and freedom. I wish I could rewind and go back at times. To sit on the couch together, unwrap Christmas presents as little kids filled with wonder, watch cartoons on the living room floor on snow days, ride the bus home from school and talk about what we learned, or run over to our friend's houses together.

Growing up, these moments and memories alongside my sister cultivated this expression of home in me. It provided the environment where community and friendship had the last word. This is why we've heard and maybe even said to someone we love, "You feel like home." To find people where intimacy and deep friendship truly exists is a rare thing. These relationships of home can only endure where people are committed to one another's flourishing.

It took some time for me to realize this concept that home is more about the people you're with than the place you live. The people we live alongside create the experiences and memories we associate with this feeling of home. It's that feeling when the family gathers around the hearth and Christmas tree alight with bulbs, ornaments, ribbon, and wreaths. It's the joy in your gut when you meet a couple friends down the street to grab a cookies and cream milkshake on a random weeknight. It's the satisfying comfort of friends laughing and lingering around a table after the meal has been eaten and the bill is paid. It's the butterflies fluttering in your chest while you sit with someone you love under the dark dome of glittering starlight.

Home is embodied where companionship and wonder meet. It's found in environments of close vulnerability, accountability, and curiosity. It's rooted in love and expressed through outlets of joy, adventure, and compassion. I had to gain new perspectives in order to learn that everybody aches to belong, and that kinship only endures when people care deeply for one another. It exists where people close in proximity share their lives together for heavenly purposes.

I think this is why people move to a new city thinking it'll solve their relational problems (and are quickly let down when it doesn't). They put too much stock in the physical address than the neighbors around them. As soon as they arrive, they realize the new city is just another spot on the map, and their relational needs are unmet. I'm a firm believer in people over places.

I began to recognize the importance of companionship during my time in college. I was able to look back at how relationships impacted my life in high school and project how they could influence my future. Wildly enough, God gave me a handful of incredible high school friends with a vision of wrapping our lives together.

Jesus changed and transformed a handful of us in our teenage years. These same relationships grew steadily over time and as high school ended we made promises to move to the same college town together. We loved what Jesus had done in our lives together and wanted to trust him with the next horizon.

Our time in college held the same richness, but with more weight and depth because of the history we had cultivated together. It wasn't anything glamorous or Hollywood-worthy. It was simple living. We devoured dining halls, went to social gatherings, dances, and sporting events, volunteered, pulled all-nighters, failed classes, dated and broke up, lived together, went to the gym, and shopped for groceries. Life was ordinary. Yet, in all the common living we experienced, our lives orbited around the same central thing. Life and union with Jesus.

Our friendships were rooted in full life. Built upon the notion that our stories would be wonderful and terrifying at times, but we had one another to experience it with. We asked each other the hard questions. We spurred one another on toward intimacy with Christ.

We encouraged each other with the hope of God when life was overwhelming. The trajectory of our friendships was aimed toward helping each other become the best, most Christ-centered versions of ourselves. We longed for one another to know Jesus deeply and for our lives to reflect it.

My college years rolled by, and life changed quite a bit. Fast forward a few years to when my wife Lindsey and I were married, still experiencing the same desire to be loved and a part of a faithful community of believers. A lot was different. I was living in a new city, had a new job, and was no longer a single person mainly concerned with myself anymore. The same old longing I had for companionship and deep connection with people lingered on.

We've now lived in a couple different cities since those early days of marriage. I can say without fail that in those different stages of moving, we often felt the inward tug and ache for a sense of home. Experiences that reinforced the notion of people over places. That inward gravity pulling toward rhythms and intimacy with people we love. Regardless of where life has carried us, we constantly face the longing for an environment to be ourselves and receive love.

Even in the commonplace of everyday life, we have the gift of engaging relationships around us. We can experience deep relationships with our friends, family, colleagues, or classmates. Companionship that was designed by our Creator to bring us joy, union, and hope. When Lindsey and I travel every so often for longer periods of time, we always notice toward the end of the trip our excitement to get back to the people we hold dear. A sure sign that we were designed for life within community that deepens our souls in Jesus.

This ache for home reflects what I believe to be a longing for fellowship as it was intended to be. An ownership of common relationships and affections stirred by the God of Creation. Life blemished but received in love.

The scriptures are very clear on the importance, if not the necessity, of life in community. Paul in his letter to the church in Thessalonica writes: "Therefore encourage one another and build one another up, just as you are doing" (1 Thessalonians 5:11 ESV). John also emphasizes this when he says: "We proclaim to you what we have seen and heard, so that you also may have fellowship with us. And our fellowship is with the Father and with his Son, Jesus Christ" (1 John 1:3 NIV).

It was essential to the early followers of the Way that, "They devoted themselves to the apostles' teaching and to fellowship, to the breaking of bread and to prayer" (Acts 2:42 NIV). At its core, our longing for relationships is rooted in God's words at creation that it is not right for man to be alone. And so, ever since our exile east of Eden, our lives have pulled back homeward. Even our prayers point to our longing for things to be as they once were. It's a beautiful picture of our hope for all things made new.

Eden was and remains the ultimate expression and environment of home. Everything in the garden was the way God lovingly created life to be. Relationships were wholesome and fulfilling. Man and woman were face to face with God, enjoying his fellowship and intimacy. It was the master's design. The blueprint for relationships and connection. An atmosphere blossoming with the fruit of closeness and intimacy.

Unfortunately, the next part of the story unfolded, and sin entered the cosmos, causing the painful fracture we feel in our lives and relationships today. Since then, all of creation has been living in exile instead of our true home with God. Tolkien, one of my favorite authors, famous for The Lord of the Rings, spoke profoundly about our wandering when he wrote, "We all long for Eden, and we are constantly glimpsing it: our whole nature at its best and least corrupted, its gentlest and most human, is still soaked with the sense of exile."[2]

We are living out our stories in exile, filled with a deep longing for Eden—life as it once was. Perfect, undivided, and unashamed union with God. Instead, now we live with all the cruelty, separation, and brokenness from the fall. In this tiring and disorienting world, we are continually assailed with opposition and hardship. Life is overwhelming at times. We can barely catch our breath. Our stories ache for things to be made right.

Jesus offers comfort to his followers when he promised, "I have told you these things so that in me you may have peace. In this world, you will have trouble. But take heart! I have overcome the world" (John 16:33 NIV). These words from Jesus have profound implications for our stories. Jesus shares this encouragement with his closest friends, and I believe it is through friendship that these words are lived out and experienced.

The counteracting agent in a grueling and crushing world is good company. It is deeper than just having friends, meeting up for drinks, going on travels, or sharing conversation with a neighbor. Although those are all elements of vibrant relationships, the purpose and power of community is most powerful when we bear each other's lives. The Apostle Paul encourages us to, "Carry each other's burdens, and in this way you will fulfill the law of Christ" (Galatians 6:2 NIV).

Fulfilling the word and purposes of God is achieved in our lives through deep heartfelt connection—and connection where we aren't repelled by the messiness and sin in one another but drawn closer because of it. We enter each other's lives and commit to encouragement, support, and gentleness. It involves reassuring each other of God's love and grace toward us. Timothy Keller speaks of this commitment to one another in his words, "Friendship is a deep oneness that develops when two people, speaking the truth in love to one another, journey together to the same horizon."[3]

The believer's horizon is Eden, the renewal of all things. As we journey through life with the backdrop of exile, we cling to one another through friendship and community. We speak truth to each other in love and lift each other up towards Jesus. We do this because we know there are so many things in this life seeking to tear us down and break us like water on rock.

True friendship wrapped around Jesus makes the veil between us and heaven that much thinner. Christ-centered friendship orbits around union with God during the everyday moments of life. It is through deep community that we are shaped and defended by those we love and love us in return. Scripture edifies in the book of Proverbs that we are to sharpen one another (Proverbs 27:17). There is no doubt our hearts are transformed and shepherded by friendship. For better or worse.

True friendship as Charles Spurgeon once said is like,

> "Having once given his heart to his chosen companion he clings to him in all weathers, fair or foul; he loves him nonetheless because he becometh poor, or because his fame suffers an eclipse, but his friendship like a lamp shines the brighter, or is made more manifest because of the darkness that surrounds it. True friendship is not

fed from the barn-floor or the winefat; it is not like the rainbow dependent upon the sunshine, it is fixed as a rock and firm as granite, and smiles superior to wind and tempest. If we have friendship at all, brethren and sisters, let this be the form it takes: let us be willing to be brought to the test of the wise man, and being tried, may we not be found wanting. A friend loveth at all times."[4]

So let us invest deeply in true Christ-like community. Connecting with the people that create our present sense of home as we walk towards our heavenly home, remembering that Jesus said, "And if I go and prepare a place for you, I will come back and take you to be with me, that you also may be where I am" (John 14:3 NIV). Indeed, let us enjoy one another and experience the heavenly fruit of friendship. Knowing that what we cultivate here will continue into eternity.

Chapter Five

Markings of Mercy

The man I looked at in the mirror this morning seems like a stranger to me. So much has changed in my complexion over the years. There are more imperfections, marks, and blemishes on my face than I can ever remember. The texture and tightness of my skin is slacker and rougher than I recognize. My eyes still seem to have their caramel hue, but they look tired and cloudy. The hair on my head resembles its hickory brown, but the occasional twinge of gray grows here and there. So much has changed in my complexion over the years that I don't recognize daily. It usually takes years before I'll wake up and notice I've aged and changed.

I have a line stretching across the bridge of my nose from where I broke it during a boating accident in my twenties. I have a Harry-Potter-like scar on my forehead from an unexpected collision during early childhood. I have a scar on my temple from slamming my head into the point of a handrail from a bike accident in middle school. It's been years since puberty, but I still have scars from teenage acne etched in my skin.

The face I see in the mirror surprises me. The longer I linger under the incandescent glow of the vanity light, the more I recognize I'm not who I once was. For better or worse, each mark on my body evokes some sort of emotion. They subtly prompt me to reflect, to consider my life, the decisions I've made, what has happened to me, and who I've become. Our scars and imperfections tell a story.

These outward markings have inward impressions. They are stories of our humanity—moments when we've wounded ourselves and reflections of when we've hurt others. There is outward bodily damage and there is affliction of the spirit. They're different, but often intertwined.

A person can have a wounded spirit without showing any evidence on the outside. These inward marks on the spirit are heartfelt reminders of tragedy, trauma, and sorrow. They are blemishes of brokenness bearing a world of emotion. They are signs of moments and experiences we often wish we could forget. Some of them are given from honest causes, but those are few and far between.

If we're honest, the pain that lies below the surface is overwhelming at times. Deep aching in our souls is often caused from sensitive moments in our lives when someone or something hurt us. There may be a physical reminder of the occurrence, but that might not be the case. There may just be the spiritual and emotional damage that lingers on. We can find ways to nurse the visible defects, but there's no quick fix to working through the inward baggage. The cruel and terrible ways of this fallen world often mark us without touching our skin. Words, experiences, and subliminal messages can wreak havoc in our stories without any visible trace.

The phrase "chicks dig scars" was popularized in a sports comedy called The Replacements starring Keanu Reeves. I first saw it in the early 2000s with my dad on the big rear-projection television in our living room. It's a sports-themed comedy centered on a football player named Shane Falco who, at the end of the film, is trying to rally his team to win the last and biggest game of the season. In Hollywood fashion, he rallies the team together and fires them up by shouting, "Pain heals. Chicks dig scars. Glory lasts forever."[1]

As a young boy, I clung to this bravado and gave a roaring hurrah! Years later, I realize the ego and ignorance from that quote is insanely callous and deceptive, yet our culture nowadays acts like it's the gospel. The actual truth about that quote is that people can deal with pain and heartache years after an experience; it's easier to cover up trauma than deal with it, and worldly glory is fragile in the end.

I've gotten my fair share of heart-level scars, and for many years, I hated how they made me feel. I wanted to pull them off like Band-Aids. I wanted the heartache to subside from those words said to me in middle school. I didn't want to live with the remorse from unkind ways I treated girls in high school. I hated the regret in my heart for specific ways I failed and let people down. I couldn't stand the grief when my friend took his own life. Life has dealt some excruciating blows and I used to think the pain and scars were something staining my life. Now I know they hold heavenly purpose and tell a story of redemption and goodness.

I've come to notice that most folks place a lot of importance on presenting their lives as picture perfect. We've become incredibly caught up in making our stories look more glamorous than they really are. It's everywhere you look. Sign on to social media and you'll notice the facade people are hiding behind.

Humans will spin things in order to communicate the most impressive version of themselves. Countless pictures and posts fluffing life up. Let's also not forget about the billion-dollar industries profiting off promises to mask our true lives.

We don't want people to know us for who we truly are because we fear rejection. Nowadays, pretending to have your life together is more applauded than actually being content with living the life you've been given. People in our current culture seem to be more captivated by portraying something inaccurate about themselves than confidently accepting the character flaws and imperfections they possess. Authenticity is slowly fading away.

I mentioned beforehand that I have this Harry-Potter-like scar on the center of my forehead, which taught me a significant life lesson about Jesus. I obtained the scar from an accident in the shoe section of a local Belk department store that epitomized the 1990s. Belk was stocked with merchandise like acid-washed jeans, Chicago Bulls apparel, Sony Discmans, and the latest Doc Martens boots.

My mother and sister were doing some back-to-school shopping, and I was asked to wait around. My interest in being patient was wearing out while the vast possibilities before me were tantalizing. If you give a five-year-old boy enough freedom, he'll find a way to entertain himself forever.

After fighting off an imaginary super villain and rescuing a damsel in distress, I made my way over to an old pocket-spring sofa squeezed in between the shoe displays. I started to use the couch as a springboard to launch my body across the room. I would pretend to calculate the distance to clear the gap, take a step back, and catapult myself from one couch to another.

I sent myself flying all around the shoe department. It was risky and thrilling—everything a young kid gets excited about. In typical fashion, I found more and more ways to contort and throw my body from couch to couch, over the display cases like I was an Olympian going for gold.

I'm convinced little boys are hardwired for trouble, and my moment came violently into focus. I configured a sequence of jumps borderline impossible to land, yet everything in my seven-year-old mind didn't count the cost. With my eyes closed, I began the countdown.

My heart was beating out of my chest and blood was pumping through my veins. I leaned forward, started my run, bent my legs, and leapt into the air. I was high enough but didn't have the distance. My feet missed the ledge, my shins hit the edge, I flipped forward, bounced sideways, and slammed my head into the corner of a show table. The impact cut the skin on my face open immediately and blood began pouring from the wound.

You would've thought a bomb went off in the store between the sound of me crashing through the shoe stand and the shrieks of people nearby who witnessed the whole thing. My sister came sprinting over with one shoe still on her foot and my mother right behind her. The nearby shoppers and employees were absolutely shocked at the scarlet scene in front of them, but this wasn't my mom's first rodeo. She had raised me over the past seven years and knew the experiences that came with it.

Mom entered the chaos unfazed and composed as most mothers seem to be in the circus of raising kids. She placed one hand on the back of my head, pressed my shirt against the cut with the other, lifted me onto my feet, told me everything would be alright, and then rushed me to the hospital. An experience that turned out to be one of the scariest nights of my childhood. A night filled with regret, an emergency room, tears, stitches, and a whole lot of pain.

I still have the scar on my forehead over twenty years later and for some odd reason it reminds me of my childish decision to run off on my own. It reminds me of my youthful longing for mischief and gravity towards trouble. To a degree, the scar on my face reflects my heart to disobey. Years later, as I stare into the mirror, I'm subtly overcome with a twinge of disappointment. This is just one of many other pain points that I've wrestled with over the years.

Pain points can be traced back in one way or another to human sinfulness. This fallen world has a way of leaving us battered and bruised. We have the terrifying ability to harm and be harmed. We are either holding the knife or the one inflicting the wound. Scars are received and given. We have caused pain in others and have hurt ourselves.

A parent walks out the door bent on a better life, leaving their family devastated. A spouse initiates an affair to fill a void. Someone exploits another person in an abusive and unhealthy relationship. A kid on the playground crumbles in tears after insults are hurled from a bully. A breakup crushes a person hoping for a partner.

The conflicts in our stories and those around us are terribly endless. And unless healing occurs, the actions of a wounded person will likely cause other experiences of hurt. All of us have probably heard a variation of the "hurting people will hurt other people" phrase. If we boil down our experiences and disappointments, we'll often realize those heart-level markings come from human brokenness.

There must be another way for us to live our lives. There must be some sort of hope and healing for our bruised and battered souls. There must be an antidote for the deeper pain of the human heart where our emotions sit hardened by the outside world. A hardness that is hard to reach and even tougher to breakthrough, especially when we've spent years locking ourselves away.

For to love is to be vulnerable, and to be vulnerable is to open ourselves up to the possibility of pain. This is the frontier of the human heart. We put our lives out into relationships, friendships, work, play, and recreation. When we give ourselves over to people and things in love, we give them the ability to hurt and harm us. It is significant for the health of the spiritual heart to connect and commune with things of this world. We were made in such a way. However, the very things we become vulnerable with have the power to cause us pain if handled without care and compassion. C.S. Lewis in The Four Loves says,

> "To love at all is to be vulnerable. Love anything and your heart will be wrung and possibly broken. If you want to make sure of keeping it intact you must give it to no one, not even an animal. Wrap it carefully round with hobbies and little luxuries; avoid all entanglements. Lock it up safe in the casket or coffin of your selfishness. But in that casket, safe, dark, motionless, airless, it will change. It will not be broken; it will become unbreakable, impenetrable, irredeemable. To love is to be vulnerable."[2]

This is one of the great tensions we hold in our lives. Do we open ourselves up to be wrung and possibly broken, or do we wrap our hearts carefully round with things that'll protect us? How we answer this question is how we'll live out our stories.

We find in Jesus the only one with the capacity and power to bring true healing in our souls. The hands of our Maker are gentle and strong, able to offer the deep redemption and restoration our wounded hearts need. The Psalmist encourages us to, "Cast your cares on the Lord and he will sustain you; he will never let the righteous be shaken." (Psalm 55:22 NIV). It is also comforting that, "The LORD is close to the brokenhearted and saves those who are crushed in spirit" (Psalm 34:18 NIV). And we should not quickly forget, "He heals the brokenhearted and binds up their wounds" (Psalm 147:3 NIV).

One of my favorite stories of Jesus occurs on the sand-swept shores of the sea of Galilee in the Gospel of Mark. Jesus, followed by his disciples, steps on land one afternoon into the chaotic life of a man possessed by a demon. Scripture doesn't address every detail of this man's story, but conjecture points towards his earlier life as any other normal person. A man who may have built sandcastles as a young boy in the very place that now haunts him with demons. A man who once had a family, friends, dreams, and hopes for his future, but somewhere along the way was taken hostage by evil spirits.

Jesus cunningly steps into the chaos and brokenness of this man, unafraid of the circumstances and fueled by love. Jesus knew this man's pain and intended to restore him. We don't know the backstory of the possessed man, or what led him to such a wretched place, but we do know Jesus didn't plan on leaving him there. For in a wild and terrifying encounter, Jesus frees the man of his bondage that has haunted him for far too long. The great waves of God's goodness and mercy crash upon this man. His life is redeemed and set free.

We are left with one last picture as the curtain closes on this account. A scene of hope, which is offered to us by Jesus as it was to this man. Mark describes the end of the event through the eyes of the townspeople, "When they came to Jesus, they saw the man who had been possessed by the legion of demons, sitting there, dressed and in his right mind; and they were afraid" (Mark 5:15

NIV). For the man who had been wounded, counted as good as dead, was sitting at the feet of Jesus, dressed in clothes, and in his right mind.

The same person who had been lost to affliction and suffering was now coherent and lucid. He was aware of grace—freed from the brokenness and evil that had kept him captive! Cured! It was a miracle that left the people frightened. The healing shocked the countryside because it was so life altering and redemptive.

I do wonder how long the possessed man had lived his life in that haze of misery and pain. I imagine him waking from his demonic slumber every so often only to be reminded nothing had changed and he may be trapped forever. Little did he know that one day on the shores below him, the King of Creation would stride across the ocean tide with one thing in mind for that man, redemption.

We too are given access to the grace and healing found in the gentle and ferocious heart of God. For he offers the mending we so desperately need. The sooner we break free from our bondage the sooner we'll step into the glorious lives God has prepared for us.

I've let experiences define who I am for many years, and I've even allowed the baggage from those experiences the power to hold my heart hostage. I've put myself out there and been cut down and rejected. I've made some terrible mistakes. I've held onto way too much for way too long. Just like how a rather unfortunate moment in a Belk department store left me scarred for life.

Regardless of magnitude, all experiences in our lives have the capacity to mark us for better or worse. What speaks most loudly to me now is no longer the remorse behind my scars but how the love of Jesus rushes in to bring healing, grace, and redemption. Like my mother scooping me into her arms, Jesus longs to be the caretaker of our bruised and beat-up hearts.

We may develop some heartache and scars along the way, but we must remember that no great adventure goes without conflict. The baggage we bear is never too heavy for the Lord to carry and unburden us from. To love is to be vulnerable. Scars speak loudly of courage and grace.

I guess that's the thing about scars—they are a subtle reminder of how far we've come, but also how much more healing we truly need. Let's not forget the most beautiful scars of all, the ones Jesus bears on his body for us. For by his wounds we are healed (Isaiah 53:5).

Chapter Six

Red Ryder Redemption

It's December again and our fire is burning in the hearth. The smell of wood, ash, and pine fill the house. Nat King Cole's Christmas record plays softly through the speakers. Our family loves rewatching some of the classic movies over the holiday season. Next on the list is A Christmas Story. The film narrates the life of the main character, Ralphie, pleading with his parents for only one thing at Christmas: a Red Ryder Carbine Action 200-shot Range Model air rifle. Unfortunately, to Ralphie's dismay, the resounding response to his Christmas wish becomes the movie's most quotable line, "You'll shoot your eye out."[1]

At the end of the movie, on Christmas morning, when it appears all the presents have been opened, Ralphie finds one last box hidden in the corner, which contains the rifle. He eagerly rushes outside, attaches a target to a metal sign, and pulls the trigger. When he fires the gun, it ricochets back and hits him in the face. Luckily enough, he realizes the BB only knocked his glasses off. The warning that Ralphie would shoot his eye out nearly came true. Sometimes the things we crave most in life end up doing the most damage.

There's something thrilling for young kids about holding a toy weapon. If a kid doesn't have the real thing, they'll fashion something out of nothing. It doesn't matter if it's a branch in the backyard, a tool from a parent's workshop, or a paper towel roll. Young kids have a way of wielding something. However, there comes an age when most kids graduate from the toy stuff to something more realistic. Like Ralphie, I also grew up begging my parents for an air rifle.

On my eighth birthday, they bought me a Red Ryder rifle. I remember the cold metal frame weighing heavy in my hands. The light reflected off the stock and assembly when I opened the box. It made my young heart race.

This rifle was an open door to new adventures. I was the backyard cowboy ruling over my rugged wilderness and I spent months shooting the new rifle and perfecting my skills. I became good enough to hit anything about 100 feet away with those little copper-coated BB pellets.

Our house in Roanoke was mostly surrounded by woods. The backyard was flat for some distance and then sloped downwards through brush toward a shallow creek bed in the lower hills. There were no houses directly behind ours, but there were a few out front. I was allowed to venture anywhere with the gun in the backyard, but the front lot was off limits for obvious reasons (breakable windows, neighbors, and passing cars).

I was naive of the boundaries set for me. The backyard was familiar territory, but the front was unconquered lands. I was cautious but wanted a new thrill and challenge. One afternoon, while everyone in my family was tied up with other things, I snuck around to the front yard and army crawled through my mother's flower bed for cover.

I lay prone with the Red Ryder stock under my right arm. Taking in my surroundings, I noticed my neighbor's bird feeder shaking slightly in the summer wind. It hung from an eastern white pine on the end of our property that was a little over a hundred feet away—the same distance I had mastered with the rifle.

I sat quietly and watched my surroundings. Nothing moved for quite some time. The whole countryside seemed to be still and silent on a midsummer afternoon. After a few minutes, a Northern Cardinal, as hefty and red as ever, floated and landed on the hanging feeder.

I remember the bird sporting a sharp crest on its chest and warm red accents. The bright red tint of its wings and body stood out among the trees. The cardinal sat pecking at the birdfeeder oblivious to the boy in the flower bed.

I didn't think of the consequences. My act against nature came suddenly and swiftly. I gave the rifle a few pumps, brought the sight to my eye, took a deep breath, and pulled the trigger. The cardinal went limp and tumbled from the feeder without making a sound. It seemed to fall in slow motion and then it rested upon the grass.

I ran over in shock with all sorts of emotions rushing into my mind. My stomach fell through my feet. A heat began to bubble in my body. A mixture of fear and shame. I snatched the dead bird and frantically placed it in my pocket. Not only had I broken the rules, but I had just taken the life from a beautiful living thing. The first living creature I had ever killed in my life.

I panicked, ran into the backyard, threw the Red Ryder across the yard, and made my way inside. I felt like a fraud, cheating the bird of its life while altogether disobeying my parents. I walked into the house right past my family with the bird bleeding in my pocket. I'd done something wrong in secret and just hoped nobody noticed me.

I should've left the poor thing outside or at least buried it, but everything caught me off guard and I panicked. I had no clue what I was doing, so I hid the bird inside a box in my sock drawer. Guilt started to rise to the surface. The consequences started to become very real. I had to keep this a secret, or I'd lose the rifle, or worse, I'd be grounded.

I left the cardinal decaying in the box for weeks. I had smuggled the dying bird into the house and couldn't risk taking it back out. Regardless of how much I tried, I couldn't come to terms with what to do with the bird. The shame I felt as a little boy weighed heavy in my chest. I had killed something, albeit a very small thing, but wonderfully beautiful, nonetheless. On top of that, I had outright disobeyed my folks.

The box began to smell, the blood pooled, and the bird simply dried out. It took a couple weeks, but one day my mom traced the odor of the little bird right to the dresser. The truth about what I had done came to light. I was found guilty. Exposed for what I had done and the boundaries I had crossed. The guilt and cowardice in my heart was on full display for everyone in my family to see.

It's been over twenty years since this memory, but I still remember sitting on the couch and realizing the profound truth of my sin. I could cause something and someone pain. It was one of the first times in my life when I truly realized the legitimacy and implications of my own sinful decisions. I began to recognize the reality I was experiencing and how sin was affecting all parts of who I was as a person.

Not much has changed over the years. I still don't know what to do with my sin at times. My tendency is to run from exposure. I want to hide the brokenness in me. I don't want to admit what is going on inside, and I surely don't want anyone to find out.

If you really knew my heart, you'd be terrified at what you'd find. If you only knew how terrible my thoughts can be at times. If you only knew how much I've struggled with anxiety and insecurity in my life. If you only knew what anger and wickedness existed inside me at times. You'd be repulsed at what you'd find.

Over the years, I've wrestled with my sin, questioned so much about myself, and wondered what to do with the twistedness. The Bible describes sin as direct violation and rebellion against God's law and design for life (1 John 3:4). The penalty for breaking God's design is death (Romans 3:23). That's a hard pill to swallow, but don't we want a world where justice is settled against the offender? Are we to think any differently about God's design and boundaries for our own lives? Sin entered the world through one man (Romans 5:12) and since then we all have fallen short of God's glory (Romans 6:23). This is the truth that's haunted human history.

The sad reality is that we've become so nonchalant with sin that we don't handle it with the seriousness it deserves. Sin is not a petty idea to meddle with or a condition to coddle. It is a very real state of our hearts that is completely destructive to our stories.

St. Augustine said in his confessions, "But my sin was this, that I looked for pleasure, beauty, and truth not in him but in myself and his other creatures, and the search led me instead to pain, confusion, and error."[2] Timothy Keller also says that, "Sin isn't only doing bad things; it's more fundamentally making good things into ultimate things."[3] And Erwin McManus wrote that, "Sin creates the illusion of freedom. In the end it fools us into seeking freedom from God rather than finding freedom in God."[4] Sin is both a condition of the heart and an abuse of our actions.

And so, it is foolish to treat sin lightly, leave it unchecked, and let it pollute our lives to the point of death. The heart must wake up and turn to God's love; it must reckon with the implications of sin and the grandeur of grace. Scripture speaks of the love of God coming crashing down in the person of Jesus to free us from our bondage to sin. The Apostle Paul encourages us with,

> And you were dead in the trespasses and sins in which you once walked, following the course of this world, following the prince of the power of the air, the spirit that is now at work in the sons of disobedience—among whom we all once lived in the passions of our flesh, carrying out the desires of the body and the mind, and were by nature children of wrath, like the rest of mankind. But God, being rich in mercy, because of the great love with which he loved us, even when we were dead in our trespasses, made us alive together with Christ—by grace you have been saved—
>
> (Ephesians 2:1-5 ESV)

This is an utter relief for a lost and fallen world. God has ransomed us back to himself. Through the life, death, and resurrection of Jesus, we are saved and brought back into deep union with God. Restoring our hearts and repurposing our lives. God's rich mercy and great love has made us alive with Jesus—simply because of grace that we are redeemed. Tim Keller says, "The gospel is this: We are more sinful and flawed in ourselves than we ever dared believe, yet at the very same time we are more loved and accepted in Jesus Christ than we ever dared hope."[5]

C.S. Lewis wrote that, "The great thing to remember is that, though our feelings come and go, His love for us does not. It is not wearied by our sins, or our indifference; and, therefore, it is quite relentless in its determination that we shall be cured of those sins, at whatever cost to us, at whatever cost to Him."[6] Jesus is not repelled by our sin or our indifference to sin. He simply doubles down and loves us even more. In gentleness and kindness, he restores us.

When we surrender and receive God's love for us, we enter new life. God reassures us that, "I will give you a new heart and put a new spirit in you; I will remove from you your heart of stone and give you a heart of flesh" (Ezekiel 36:26 NIV). The prophet Jeremiah also writes, "I will give them a heart to know that I am the LORD, and they shall be my people and I will be their God, for they shall return to me with their whole heart" (Jeremiah 24:7 ESV).

And so, with a new heart and new purpose for living we return to God. We throw off everything that hinders, the sin that so easily entangles, and we fix our eyes on Jesus. We engage a more abundant life than that which was forfeited by sin, more wonderful than we could ever imagine.

Understanding that we'll grow more and more into our glorified selves as sin diminishes in us. Realizing that even in our errors, we are beloved by God. For Jesus does not expect sinless perfection but does warn against a return to a sinful lifestyle. His words extend both mercy and claim holiness. A faithful life is the right balance of grace and truth.

I think it's worth noting that in many Christian circles, there tends to be more emphasis placed on sin than the newness and belovedness we experience in surrendering to Jesus. We've become blinded to our own radiance in Christ because of a fixation on transgressions. While our sin tendencies will remain, let's not forget that we are saints because of Jesus. We are new creatures. The Apostle Paul reassures us that, "Therefore, if anyone is in Christ, he is a new creation. The old has passed away; behold, the new has come" (2 Corinthians 5:17 ESV).

Paul is reminding us of the assurance of God's glory and grace. He is pointing to the true heart that exists in the surrendered life made new in Jesus. There is a significant distinction between sinful tendencies and the authentic life remade in Christ. We must recognize that in Jesus our hearts are renewed, reborn, and made glorious. John Eldredge, in his book Waking the Dead, pens, "God endowed you with a glory when he created you, a glory so deep and mythic that all creation pales in comparison. A glory unique to you, just as your fingerprints are unique to you, just as the way you laugh is unique to you. Somewhere down deep inside we've been looking for that glory ever since."[7]

This is the glory of a heart fully alive: becoming more and more restored into its rightful shape as God intended. And while sin and brokenness will still be a part of the story, we have what we need in Jesus to engage in a truly remarkable life. We find fulfillment through Jesus and can experience union with God here and now. Freedom is found when we let go of sin and cling to Christ. Holiness will become more of the natural reflex.

Not only that, but if I'm being honest, it is a great comfort to be able to look back over the course of human history and recount the number of heroes of our faith who dropped the ball.

To be able to look at the stories of some of the saints and realize they wanted to give up at times. To know that David was an adulterer, murder, and liar. Peter a betrayer. Jacob was a deceiver. Solomon a lustful idolater. Paul was titled the "chief of sinners."

We can feel right at home amongst all those screw-ups. If love abounds for all those broken people, then there is great hope and assurance for you and me. What a comforting truth to know God's love extends to us just as it did to the countless individuals in Scripture who seemed to blow it every chance they got.

It means we're not alone. It means that through God's grace, there is great company amongst fellow believers. There is an invitation for us to sit at the master's table that has been offered to thousands before us and will continue after us.

The call is full of welcome and thanksgiving. To eat and drink of his forgiveness and hope. His cup, sweet and strong, touches all our lips with electric love. His body, full of power and might, broken for you and me to experience abounding grace.

One of the ways we can engage God in the everyday moments of life is by professing our deep need for Jesus. It is communing with God, acknowledging our waywardness, and allowing him to realign our hearts. It is becoming more aware of the playfulness and gentleness of Jesus drawing the sin out of our lives.

It is actively engaging the Spirit of God as we're taking out the trash, sitting in traffic, waiting at the mechanic, or washing the car. It is surrendering everything and everyone to God throughout the day so he can restore our union with him.

Jesus invites us into his overflowing goodness where we can live with deeply rich faith, but we need to understand the inner workings of our lives. Freedom comes through acknowledging our shortcomings, admitting that sin pollutes all parts of our stories, and clinging to the atoning work of Jesus.

Sin was lurking in my heart when I disobeyed my parents with the Red Ryder rifle. It brought me shame as the dead bird bled out in my pocket. Sin rotted in my consciousness like the creature in my sock drawer. Yet, great relief came when everything was brought to light—when the bird was finally found, and my sinfulness was reckoned with. There was great goodness experienced through acknowledging my wrongdoings.

The same is true in our relationship with Jesus. It is only through his love that we experience the redemption and rescue we so desperately need. The ability to become more alive and forgiven than we ever dared dreamed.

God has won our lives back to himself through Jesus. Restoring our hearts and repurposing our lives. Through him, we have an invitation into a new life of brilliance. A life overflowing.

Chapter Seven

We Few, We Happy Few

We packed up Quentin's red Chevy Tahoe the summer break after our Junior year of college and headed west towards George Washington National Forest. Four of us decided at the last minute to go camping, so we threw together the fireside essentials: hot dogs, Miller Light, and stuff for s'mores. If the police pulled us over, it would've looked more like we were heading east to a beach town than a campground. All of us were wearing tank tops, boardshorts, and Vans skate shoes.

We pulled into Breeden Bottom mid-afternoon as the countryside turned shades of emerald and basil in the summer sun. We ditched the Tahoe and made for the James River. There was a rope swing on the northern bank that could throw you halfway across the water if you timed it right. The water was kept cool in a canopy of shade from the willow and pine trees lining the riverbank. We played, wrestled, and rested for hours. The sun began its unfailing decent west, which signaled it was time to set up camp.

We were all in charge of specific responsibilities for the trip, and mine was to bring the tent. In a rush earlier that day, I scrambled through my dad's camping gear and snagged the tent equipment without checking what was in the bag. Our campground came to life as Landon and Tim got the fire started and Quentin and I assembled the tent. The evening began to glow, the sky turned ginger and crimson, and we settled in by the fireside telling stories.

Eventually, we turned in for the night, grabbed our sleeping bags, and fell off to sleep in the tent under an umbrella of stars. The night turned dark and cold, and at some point, I woke up as rain drops started to hit the canvas above our heads. I immediately realized that we hadn't assembled the rain cover over the tent because it wasn't in the bag. I had left it at home.

The rest of the guys stirred awake as I frantically covered the tent on the outside with towels, shirts, and an umbrella, anything to stop the water from coming directly through the mesh liner of the tent. It was pointless. No matter what we tried, the rain found its way into the tent, down the sides of the walls, and onto the floor. We eventually gave up, slipped back into our sleeping bags, and surrendered to the rain.

We woke up several hours later as the sun crawled over the mountains and the robins began their songs. It was a lovely morning beckoning us into another day of adventure, but unfortunately the inside of the tent told a different story. Everything was soaked, and everyone was drenched.

Landon was in a pool of water submerged in his sleeping bag. Our clothes, bookbags, and camping gear were ruined. We planned to stay a couple more days, but the resounding agreement was to head home because we didn't want to endure another miserable rainy night. The campground was quiet as we tossed our wet gear into the trunk.

On the way home, we grabbed breakfast at the only place we could find for several miles. I remember sitting there in the booth at Bojangles. A couple of us were still wearing wet clothes. All of us had a chill in our bones and spirits were low.

My mind was racing with all sorts of self-loathing and insecurity. I was the one who dropped the ball with the tent gear. I was the one who got us into this mess and ruined the trip. I felt like such a fool and wanted to make things right, but I was paralyzed by my emotions.

Tim was the first to laugh. It was a break in the silence. An antidote for our worn-out morale. Before we knew it, the whole booth was erupting with laughter. It was a small reflection of the moment in the Lord of The Rings when Sam Gamgee wakes up to his friend Gandalf after just being rescued from death. Tolkien writes, "At last he gasped: 'Gandalf! I thought you were dead! But then I thought I was dead myself. Is everything sad going to come untrue? What's happened to the world?' 'A great Shadow has departed,' said Gandalf, and then he laughed and the sound was like music, or like water in a parched land; and as he listened the thought came to Sam that he had not heard laughter, the pure sound of merriment, for days upon days without count. It fell upon his ears like the echo of all the joys he had ever known. But he himself burst into tears. Then, as a sweet rain will pass down a wind of spring and the sun will shine out the clearer, his tears ceased, and his laughter welled up, and laughing he sprang from his bed."[1]

In its own way, our laughter and merriment washed away the dejection we were feeling, and the whole afternoon felt lighter from that moment onward. Even the way I look back on that trip now has a different sentiment. Life often unfolds a lot like that camping trip.

It may include varying levels of adventure, danger, risk, beauty, and wonder, but hopefully it always involves friendship and community. A sigh of relief beside someone we value and hold dear. Life shouldn't unfold alone because our stories should revolve around people. Life is exceedingly more wonderful when wrapped around friends.

Friendship and fellowship have been the backdrop of life from the dawn of creation. In the first few pages of the Bible, we learn about the unifying fellowship that eternally exists amongst the Triune God. The first image of friendship we see in the cosmos. A unifying relationship that becomes the blueprint and design when God created mankind.

We are created beings that reflect and bear the image of the Godhead. The longing and desire we have for community lives in our blood and bones. To know and be known. To love and love in return. It is a direct reflection of the creator himself.

Without holy friendship, our lives would feel bleak. Jesus says to his disciples, "This is my commandment: Love each other in the same way I have loved you. There is no greater love than to lay down one's life for one's friends" (John 15:12-13 NLT). And the disciple John said this about life and fellowship when referring to Jesus, "We saw it, we heard it, and now we're telling you so you can experience it along with us, this experience of communion with the Father and his Son, Jesus Christ. Our motive for writing is simply this: We want you to enjoy this, too. Your joy will double our joy!" (1 John 1:3-4 MSG).

The ultimate picture of friendship is one that wraps around Jesus and extends outward. Where the reflex of the relationship is to give up your own life in order to elevate the life of the other individual. The true mark of deep Christian companionship is selflessness and humility, laying our lives down for one another, like Jesus did for us.

When you think about the endurance of believers throughout history, it is worth noting the emphasis placed on companionship and life together. The writer of Hebrews says, "And let us consider how we may spur one another on toward love and good deeds, not giving up meeting together, as some are in the habit of doing, but encouraging one another—and all the more as you see the Day approaching" (Hebrews 10:24-25 NIV). This is the anchor of rich fellowship.

The early ways of the church were founded on these principles, wrapping their lives around the gospel and community. It was a painstaking effort of trust and martyrdom fueled by the Spirit of God. Through prayer and petition, the people of Jesus lived out their lives alongside one another, extending the goodness of the gospel into a broken world. Have you ever thought about what unfolded in history in order for you to hear about Jesus?

It's a miraculous work of God that his Word even reached our ears, let alone touched our hearts. We take it for granted, but the events that unfolded, over thousands of years, for you and I to experience the gospel of Christ is extraordinary. Thank God the news of the gospel didn't wither away before it got to me.

Jesus communed with the disciples. He made friends. He interacted and engaged with strangers. We learn of God's love and design for communal living in the ways Jesus treated women, the marginalized, the powerless, the immoral, the sinners, the saints, the deaf, the paralyzed, the broken, the scorned, the prideful, the religious, the unbelievers, the rich, the comfortable, the lazy, and the confused.

It's written all over his life. Jesus steps into a person's story with the intention to heal and unify. He enters communities where others wouldn't dare step foot. He touches and befriends those that have been casted out and left for dead. He encourages those who are doubtful and wayward. Jesus continually reinforces his desire for union and intimacy through friendship.

Jesus' life is the megaphone of God's heart for humanity. It is the compass and guide for how we can live and treat one another. It is an encouragement to care for our neighbor regardless of ethnicity, bank account, job, title, relationship status, or degree. Even the way Jesus speaks and carries himself around the disciples is a way for us to learn and reflect God's design for relationships and friendships. There is depth and dependence in true heavenly friendship.

During high school, around the time I was beginning to follow Jesus, I started to meet with a few peers to talk about life, friendships, and faith. We were a patchwork of friends resembling the stereotypes of the Breakfast Club. The athlete, nerd, artist, and outcast all joined together every Wednesday morning. We would stumble under the parking lot lamps into Panera on the corner of Ogden Road, half asleep, to read Scripture together and discuss the direction of our lives.

We would slouch over half-eaten blueberry bagels and empty cups of coffee, talking about Jesus and his wonderful love for us. Our conversations revolved around God and how he offered our lives so much more. It pushed us to think about where life was taking us, how we were changing, and how we could make a difference in the world. For years, we met together, read, prayed, and dreamed of how our community of friends could encourage and bring hope to those around us.

After breakfast, we would always pile into Cliff's Toyota 4Runner and head to school. As we passed the 7-Eleven convenience store off Electric Road, Cliff made a habit of rolling the windows down, regardless of weather, and playing "Fix You" by Coldplay through the stereo. We would shout and sing the lyrics as the morning air filled our lungs and blew around our shaggy teenage hair. Each one of us would choose an imaginary instrument to play as if we were the band in front of a sold-out arena.

Tim was the pianist, Landon crushed the drums, Dan had a knack for bass, and Adam would absolutely shred the lead guitar. The song builds momentum steadily until the chorus comes crashing down at the end. If you were lucky enough to stand on the corner of Chaparral and Woodthrush, you might just catch it: Chris Martin from Coldplay along with a handful of puberty-stricken high school boys singing:

> "Lights will guide you home
> And ignite your bones
> And I will try to fix you"[2]

I tend to hyper-spiritualize things. Maybe it's because I believe everything in life is a shadow of heaven and the world to come, but either way, there's something heavenly about being guided home, coming alive, and being mended and made whole. There's something sacred and purposeful to friendship and community that reflects those song lyrics. Let's not forget that Jesus calls himself the true light of the world and even encourages his followers to bear the same image, that people may see, glorify, and know God's love (John 8:12). In community, these lyrics can flourish and find their true home in scripture.

The stories and moments that rippled outward from the Panera table remind me of the ways we're created to serve and love one another. That same group of friends in high school have, for the most part, stuck together for over fifteen years now.

We've wrapped our lives around faith in Jesus and allowed it to propel us forward. We found purpose and direction for how we wanted to shape our stories. Jesus was inviting us into a life of fullness cultivated through deeply vibrant friendships.

And even though life and proximity has changed for most of us, our viewpoint on friendship is still founded on the same ideas. We've let it overflow into new relationships and new communities. Some of us live in the same city now and go to the same church. We've been groomsmen in each other's weddings. We've walked through life and death together. We've celebrated new jobs and jobs lost. We've ridden across the United States on motorcycles. We've prayed with strangers. We've welcomed newborns into the world. Imperfectly, we've trusted Jesus with it all.

And I think that's why things have stuck together all of these years. Jesus is at the center of it, holding everything together. He allowed us to grow in friendship with one another in the first place. He established purpose and passion in our lives. He inspired us into mission and serving others. God used community to launch us into the unknown.

The paradox is that we were known in the unknown. First, we found how loved we are by Jesus, and then we began to experience it through one another. We lived with this mindset of an empty chair. We talked about who wasn't in the room with us and what we were going to do in order to get them there. The gospel of Jesus always extends to the next person.

In the play Henry V by Shakespeare, Henry the King of England urges his men who were vastly outnumbered by the French to recall how the English had previously been victorious in battle. In his speech, there are many distinct lines, but these strike a deeper chord for me:

> "We few, we happy few, we band of brothers;
> For he today that sheds his blood with me
> Shall be my brother"[3]

Scripture makes it clear that there is no greater expression of love than someone who lays down their life for others. As we partner with God in the writing of our stories, we'll learn that full life is found in the company of friends. Most of the stories we'll tell on our deathbeds are going to orbit around heavenly relationships. Hopefully the people we sit around with when we're telling those stories are the same life-long companions.

Deep, enduring impressions on our lives will come from the collective impact of friendships. Nostalgia has a way of weaving itself around a community of people. There is something beautiful and sacred about living faithfully in community and pressing that circle ever outward. Outward where we share meals together, renovate houses together, serve the poor together, care for the marginalized together, raise children together, travel together, worship together, weep together, create together, volunteer together, and love together.

Together.

We few, we happy few.

Chapter Eight

Billboard Dave

During one fall semester in college, word spread around campus that my good friend Dave was going to be the next poster boy for our school. The university was starting a new marketing campaign and needed a cheerful face on their advertisements. The original model chosen for the job backed out at the last minute and Dave somehow got the gig. The University of Mary Washington took Dave's portrait but didn't specify how they intended to use his picture for their marketing purposes. So, we lived in anticipation for months waiting for the big reveal.

Late one evening, as my buddy Landon and I were lounging at our college house, we heard a knock on the door. I opened it to Dave's big grin, which typically meant we were in for an adventure. I gave Dave a hug and invited him inside, but he quickly responded with, "Come with me fellas. I have something to show you." Without hesitation an excited "I'm in," rang across the room.

We hopped in Dave's car and headed south on Interstate 95. The car ride was bustling with anticipation and excitement. We had no clue what Dave had up his sleeve or how long we'd have to wait to find out, but several minutes into the drive, Dave looked at us and said almost through a whisper, "Boys, the university decided to use my picture on a billboard." Landon punched the dashboard with a resounding, "Let's go!" and I stuck my head out of the window yelling nonsense in amazement.

We drove south for what felt like an hour through our fidgeting and suspense. Sure enough, the billboard rose over the horizon with Dave's face stamped on the front. It was the biggest, brightest, and most colorful portrait of him I'd ever seen in my life. It wasn't the small silhouette of Dave's body we were expecting, but literally a close-up portrait of his entire face posted on the billboard. We did the math later and Dave's face equated to 672 square feet of advertising space.

Dave slammed on the brakes and veered off the side of the road in the shoulder. We hopped out of the car as tractor trailers whizzed by, hopped a couple fences, and ran out into the cold winter night, dying of laughter with tears in our eyes, Dave's dashing smile growing bigger and whiter every step of the way. There he was, one of the most secretly incredible guys we ever knew, made larger than we could ever have imagined. We climbed a ladder to the platform of the billboard to get as close as we could to take a selfie.

The incredible irony of this is that Dave doesn't need to be on a billboard to live large. He doesn't need the limelight to express who he is or how he treats people. He approaches life the other way around. He lives big and loves large in the quieter and smaller moments of everyday life. Dave doesn't need the spotlight to live a significant story.

On top of that, Dave is one of the most genuine and lionhearted guys I know that's always been in the business of leaving people better than when he found them. He's all about going out of his way to put love and grace in front of people so they can believe in it for themselves. Dave's the kind of person you always want around and never get tired of.

So many unforgettable memories in my life have involved Dave. We met in college through Young Life—the same organization I met Cliff in. Dave and I connected through the mission of reaching friends with the good news of Jesus. He wanted to help people understand the heart of God, and I was baffled at how simply he did it.

Not because he's loud or draws attention to himself, but because he loves people for who they are by showing them who Jesus is. He's more like a river to a canyon than waves to a shore—his impact is made over time. Dave subtly leaves people better than when he first finds them.

I think one of the biggest things I've learned from people like Dave over the years is how to engage faith in my day-to-day life. I used to believe I needed a huge platform to tell people about Jesus, but now I realize my life on ground level is the frontier for that. I don't need my story on a billboard to make a difference in the lives around me. Sure, plenty of folks have platforms, and that's all fine and good, but most of our lives will be behind the curtain.

The Apostle Paul expressed a similar idea when he wrote, "Make it your goal to live a quiet life, minding your own business and working with your hands, just as we instructed you before. Then people who are not believers will respect the way you live, and you will not need to depend on others" (1 Thessalonians 4:11-12 NLT). There is something wonderfully significant to living a quiet, gentle, and purposeful life.

Our stories, when they have this posture, have a way of becoming irresistible to a lost and lonely world. Through the in-and-outs of our daily lives, we can connect and commune with people without needing to be over-the-top about our spirituality. We don't have to look for extravagant things or platforms to experience God or share Jesus with those around us. We just need to step into the glory and adventure that Jesus is offering to us in our everyday lives.

What I love so much about Jesus is that during his ministry, he always moved out of the limelight. The moment all eyes were on him, he would dodge the crowd and get out of town. On countless occasions, Jesus would perform a miracle in secret and ask the person to stay quiet about it.

If anything, Jesus seemed to avoid the big stage. He was constantly living with intentionality in the smaller moments. Why is this? Wouldn't he want to make a big fuss about his life, ministry, and agenda? Maybe, we've got it all wrong. Maybe we've projected onto our spirituality and faith an incorrect way of living.

One of my favorite interactions that we read in stories about Jesus was written by John, and it's where Jesus feeds thousands of people. To me, this story pulls back the curtain on Jesus and his heart for his friends and the people around him. Jesus lets his best friends, the disciples, in on the miracle. He allows them to partake in feeding the crowd on the hillside. He welcomes them into the story with him.

Isn't it so wonderful of Jesus to invite us into life with him? It might look like getting to work on time after a chaotic morning. Shuffling the kids off to school. Having the patience to embrace a coworker who has dropped the ball. Life for us with Jesus is going to look a lot like getting through another regular day on earth. Except for the wonderful reality that we get to enjoy and experience his presence in those moments. Every menial act of our lives offers the opportunity to engage with the God of the universe.

After the crowd had witnessed God's miraculous provision, they looked to crown Jesus as king. Rightly so, they put Jesus in the spotlight because of their amazement, trying to put him on a billboard. Jesus, however, ducked out of sight and retreated into the wilderness by himself. He didn't care for the publicity or fame.

Jesus was all about loving people in the ordinary moments of life. While every miracle Jesus performed was extraordinary, most of those moments were in ordinary experiences of life. Jesus turned water into wine at a wedding. He restored a blind man's sight while traveling to Jericho. He healed countless people in passing. All done in earthly cities, with earthly people, doing earthly duties. I don't say all of this to downplay the wonder and power of Jesus' life, but rather to emphasize that he thrived by being intentional with people in regular moments of everyday life.

This is one thing I think we can learn about faith from Jesus. There are going to be some downright ordinary and mundane days ahead of you and me. Most of our stories will be insanely monotonous and common. There are hundreds of Tuesdays on the calendar in our past and there will be hundreds of them in the future.

What this means is that you and I are going to have some very vanilla days, which is perfectly alright and a wonderful reminder of our finite capacities and humanness. We don't need to run off and fill up our schedules with things to try to make it non-mundane. We also don't need to feel like our lives are somehow worse than someone else's because every moment doesn't look like a highlight reel.

Your story, in Jesus, is already more than enough and has the recipe for so much more. The key to joy, hope, and contentment is through encountering God in all the different avenues of everyday life. The brilliance of our stories is the culmination of how we spend each day.

Our stories compound through the way we spend our time. It's alright to wake up tired, fumble through breakfast, and stumble off into your day. What really matters is our awareness of how Jesus wants to speak and relate to us in those moments.

The best way to grow in our ability to stay faithful and aware of God in our everyday work and play is by discovering more of Jesus' love and purpose for those activities. The more we go into our daily lives with the hope of uncovering more of who Jesus is, the more we're going to become aware of him alongside us. The more we fix our eyes on Jesus, the more we'll realize his nearness. Most of our daily responsibilities most likely won't offer much excitement, but Jesus is purposefully at work in all of it.

Saint Irenaeus of Lyon, a Greek bishop in the second century, is attributed for saying that, "The glory of God is man fully alive."[1] A turn of phrase that totally hits the nail on the head with what I'm reflecting on. God is wonderfully exalted and adored when the heart of man and woman is fully alive. If this is true, it bears a significant weight on our hearts and in turn the richness of our stories.

If we turn the pages of Scripture, we'll read that, "Then Christ will make his home in your hearts as you trust in him. Your roots will grow down into God's love and keep you strong" (Ephesians 3:17 NLT). As a follower of Jesus, you can be sure of this: he lives in your heart. Which has massive implications on our stories as we live out our everyday lives.

There's a book called Every Moment Holy by Doug McKelvey that consists of practical prayers for day-to-day moments of life. I've often wrestled with prayer and questioned whether I'm doing it right or enough at times, but in a wonderful way, this book creates the perfect bridge. It's a simple and wonderful avenue to have written words and prayers to help connect with God in the monotony of life. One of my favorite liturgies in Every Moment Holy puts to words this ache of my heart:

> "...Teach me to shepherd the small duties
> Of this day with great love,
> Tending faithfully those tasks
> You place within my care
> And tending with patience and
> Kindness the needs and hearts of
> Those people you place within my reach..."[2]

You see we often miss what God is doing in the brief and routine moments of our everyday lives because we don't think God exists there. We tether God to Sundays at church or the occasional coffee shop heart-to-heart. However, the prayer above longs to bring God's meaning and purpose into every crevice of our lives and gives shape to the how and why.

Every Moment Holy has a prayer for just about anything. Eating a meal with friends, one for watching a sunset, for those who cannot sleep, for those who weep without knowing why, and a prayer for changing diapers. What it's taught me over the years is that God longs to bring us freedom and providence as we pursue him. These prayers have inspired me to discover Jesus' extraordinary love and goodness in the ordinary rhythms of life.

When a man once asked Jesus how to grasp this abundant life, here and now, the answer was to, "'Love the Lord your God with all your heart and with all your soul and with all your strength and with all your mind' and, 'Love your neighbor as yourself'" (Luke 10:27 NIV). It was a present reality that focuses on loving God and loving neighbor. The vertical relationship we have with Jesus empowers the horizontal relationships of our lives.

I think one of the ways to love the Lord your God with all your heart and with all your soul and with all your strength and with all your mind *is* by loving your neighbor as yourself. As we love the people around us our hearts ultimately turn toward God. It is a harmonizing relationship to love God and love neighbor. They coexist and complement each other. What I mean by this is that we can know Jesus more deeply by being his hands and feet. In knowing Jesus more deeply, we will be more inclined to love our neighbor. By loving our neighbor, we will be more inclined to love God.

Each of our stories has been crafted in particular ways by God to help others know they are both liked and loved by God. And the methods in which we extend a loving touch doesn't need to be wrapped in spirituality. It could be something as simple as snagging an extra coffee for your coworker and taking the time to listen and ask them questions about their life.

It may look like taking dinner to a family who just had a kid or lost someone they loved. It may be giving the kid who walks home from school a ride. By living into our humanity through God's kindness and grace, we embody the heart and person of Jesus. This is the simple yet profound daily act of loving your neighbor.

It's getting back to what my friend Dave does naturally. He loves people well for who they are and where they are. He never seems to have an agenda or angle. I find it ironic that out of all the people I know, Dave was the one who ended up on a billboard. The least likely person to draw attention to himself, yet the most likely to be attentive to others.

Dave is the type of person who easily makes the most of each moment he encounters. He's got this uncanny ability to recognize that life is precious, and each act of our lives is an expression of love and faith. The way you talk to your kid is an extension of your heart. How you greet your spouse when you walk in the door after a long day of work is evidence of who you're becoming.

Those small moments when our hearts or on display shows more about us than we know. As I've said before, how we spend our days is undeniably how we spend our lives. So, what we do, why we do it, and how we do it really does matter.

What I've learned over the years is that every moment really is holy, even though it may not seem like it at times. Doing the mountain of dishes in the sink is the last thing I want to do after a stressful day, but what doing those dishes conveys to my family matters. The same goes for us when we're at work, spending time with our friends, or interacting with our neighbors. The ways we approach those occurrences say so much more about our hearts and lives in Jesus than we give credit. How do you treat the mundane in your life?

After our sides hurt from laughing and cheering about the billboard, we made sure to take a picture of the life-sized Dave beside the blown-up Dave. All you could see in the picture was the 672 square feet of his face and a little tiny shadow in the bottom corner of Dave standing there in real time. Life is like that, the more we love people the way Jesus does, the more we shrink into the background. The way it's supposed to be.

The advertising company eventually tore Dave's face off the billboard for something new, but the memory lives on. Likewise, our stories can have a deep way of impacting people even if we're not in the picture anymore. Being the hands and feet of Jesus is for life-size humans, up close and personal.

How we treat people every single day is more relatable and influential than a billboard. We have the heavenly privilege of lifting others up and helping them see their innate worth in Jesus. What a joy it is to serve, encourage, and affirm another person. So let us treat the people around us with the same intentionality and care of Jesus. Knowing that life is precious, and every act of our stories is an opportunity to reflect the heart of heaven.

Chapter Nine

Strawberries and Cream

I 'll never forget sitting in the doctor's office for my physical rehabilitation appointment right after college. The subtle buzz of fluorescent lights flickering from above and the eerie silence of the empty waiting room. I couldn't dodge the war of doubt and disbelief ragging in my head.

I had been experiencing acute pain in my lower back for several years and finally scheduled time with a specialist to find a diagnosis. I had been to the doctor's office for several exams, and they were bringing me back in for another round of scans and images. Hopefully this time things would become clear, and we could have a verdict moving forward.

My legs and hands were fidgeting with anxiety and fear. My mind flooded with questions about God's plan for my life. Hundreds of thoughts were running through my mind, and I fumbled internally trying to make sense of it all. This wasn't just a crossroads for me. It wasn't just identifying whether the pain I was experiencing would persist, but rather if I'd be able to continue pursuing my dreams of professional tennis. This was a diagnosis of my dreams.

Part of uncovering your story can only be found by working through the heartbreak and disappointment that you've experienced throughout the course of your life. It is often through pain that we discover how wholesome and remarkable life can truly be. For me, a lot of disappointment in my life can be traced back to athletics. I played a handful of sports growing up, but never excelled at anything until high school when I fell in love with tennis.

The summer before my freshman year of high school, I picked up a racket for the very first time. Sure, I had picked up a racket plenty of times in my life before this, but for some reason, something magical happened this one specific time. It was a genesis moment for me. A domino that would cause other desires and dreams.

I'm sure plenty of us have experienced similar moments with various things in our lives. Where you did something, you've done before a hundred times, but for some reason it just felt more profound at one point. What was it for you?

I jumped in the car one afternoon with my dad and sister as they were leaving to go play tennis. They had been practicing a lot that summer since Lauren was competing to play on the high school team. I tagged along, needing to get out of the house and escape my summer boredom. I played baseball growing up and felt completely out of place around tennis. For most of the afternoon, I sat on the bleachers watching from a distance, but eventually something drew me out onto the court.

I can close my eyes and still recount that afternoon as if it happened last week. I remember the scent of Azalea bushes beyond the chain-link fence lingering on the summer breeze. The subtle heat radiating up off the hard-court surface into my shoes and toes.

I can picture the shadows of trees and light posts growing longer on the court as the sun dropped into the evening sky. I remember the popping sound of a can of tennis balls being cracked open. I can still smell their rubber scent. I can recall seeing the yellow ball fuzz floating in the air when it collides with the racket.

I didn't know it at the time, but at that moment, God was revealing to me a love for tennis and dreams that would revolve around it. That day was the spark of it all. I played tennis the rest of the summer as I made up my mind to enjoy this new adventure. Like anyone who starts to love something for the first time, whether a hobby or craft, I began to dive into it whole-heartedly. It became a wonderful avenue for me to exercise, compete, and learn plenty of life lessons.

I went on to play throughout high school, competitively in junior tournaments, and at a collegiate level. What started out as an aimless summer afternoon in high school turned into an audacious dream. Somewhere along the way, I developed this vision that continued to grow until it became the next horizon. It was the desire to win Wimbledon, a tennis tournament simply referred to as the Championships. It is the oldest competition in the sport and widely regarded as the most prestigious competition in the tennis world.

Wimbledon is situated in southwest London, England. It's a twenty-minute stroll from Southfields station through Wimbledon Village, lined with boutiques and chic cafes. The Championships are played every summer amongst the roar and rumble of thousands of visitors. The uniqueness of Wimbledon is rooted in its culture and customs.

The entire tournament is played on grass. Players can only wear white uniforms on the grounds. During the fortnight of the tournament, nearly 150,000 servings of strawberries and cream will be served. Spectators will sit adorned on the lawn in their British attire and enjoy the Pimm's Cup, a famous cocktail first appearing at Wimbledon in 1971. There are traditions celebrated during this event unlike any other.

My skill level had significantly escalated in college, and after graduation, I moved back home and continued to train. I registered for a membership with the International Tennis Federation for the World Tennis Tour and entered a few tournaments. I knew the odds were against me since I started playing when I was fourteen, which is the age most other professionals are starting to go on tour. I was years behind, and my chances were low, but my love and skill for the game had been growing immensely over the years. The dream was burning bright.

But there I sat, in my early twenties, waiting to see the specialist at my physical medicine and rehabilitation appointment. Wishing for the diagnosis to be good. Praying the doctor would have a solution for me to keep pursuing tennis at a highly competitive level. God wouldn't give me a dream just to take it away, would he? I had gotten my hopes up, and it was crumbling to the ground. At least at the level of competitive play I was dreaming about.

The scans came back showing scoliosis, an abnormal curvature in my spine, which had been putting significant stress on my back over the years. Depending on the severity of scoliosis, it can push the ribcage out of position and put strain on the muscles of the back, causing pain and discomfort. The pain was heightened from my frequency and longevity of training. The doctor said that I could either choose between continuing to deal with the pain of playing, which would only intensify over the years, or cut it back all together. There were no other options.

After my diagnosis, I sat in my 2001 Honda Civic for hours, crying with my head pressed against the steering wheel. The black-and-white images of my spine laying in the passenger seat. Becoming the next Wimbledon champion felt impossible. I wasn't making much ground with winning tournaments and now this dream-shattering news.

The setbacks kept mounting and the dream was fading from view. My body couldn't keep up and time wasn't on my side. My mind continued to race and fight for hope, but the hard truth began to settle over me. I had to come to terms with the death of a dream, and it was gut-wrenching.

What dreams have you had in your life that died? I'm not referring to a pipedream you may pursue down the road if life makes room for it. I'm speaking to the dream and vision you truly had to let pass because life circumstances couldn't support it. Maybe you had hopes of starting a family, but your body couldn't procreate. Maybe you were working your tail off for that big break, but for some reason it just never came.

I recently had a conversation with a good friend, and we were talking about dreams. He told me that he had a dream years ago of going fishing with his dad in Montana, but that his dad passed away before they could ever get out there. My wife Lindsey aspired to playing soccer in college, but after two torn ACLs, that dream stretched and tore away. Maybe there was a brief window in time for a dream to happen, but it simply passed. What is that desire for you?

I'd say there are hundreds of reasons, if not thousands, we could throw around here, but the principle is the same. Some dreams die. Let me say it differently. Sometimes in life, the thing you pursue and have vision for falls through. Which is a wounding and heartbreaking thing. But hear me out with this: there is life and hope on the other side of that death. Yes, sometimes our longings in life break down, but sometimes things must collapse for other things to be reborn.

As Christians, we acknowledge that resurrection only comes through death. Take the seasons for example. We are enveloped in the colors, sounds, and smells of a bright spring morning after living through the cold and gray of winter. Nature itself speaks to the power of renewal, and so do our lives.

My friend, Mike, talks a whole lot about having dreams and visions for your life. He is a big dreamer himself and always invites people into the room to dream with him. I'll never forget sitting down for tacos one day with him when he asked me, "Did you know that the apostle Paul had a dream to go on a missionary journey to Spain?" I tried thinking about the drawings inside the front of my Bible as a kid that outlined Paul's journeys but couldn't come up with a good answer.

He showed me the scriptures where Paul says, "I plan to do so when I go to Spain. I hope to see you while passing through and to have you assist me on my journey there, after I have enjoyed your company for a while" (Romans 15:24 NIV). Right after that, Mike asked me if I remembered anywhere in the Bible that might have referred to Paul ever actually setting foot in Spain. I struck out again. Mike went on to share that Paul likely never stepped foot in Spain for another missionary journey because he never explicitly said anything else about the trip. While we don't know the end of the story, we do know for sure that Paul clearly expressed his desire and dream to travel there.

I've always been struck by my conversations with Mike over the years, but that one conversation has always haunted me in a good way. Looking back now, I see the point he was trying to make as we sat there talking about our dreams. Whether or not Paul ever made it to Spain, the trip was still something that was on Paul's horizon. It was a vision he used to propel his life. I'd even like to say that it was a compass of sorts that oriented his direction. Paul had a dream, and he moved towards it.

Some of the thoughts that I keep asking myself are this, does God care deeply about our dreams and desires? Is the King of the universe attentive and gracious with the desires of our hearts?

Did he give us imaginations to envision a brighter future? Did God give us brilliance and intellect to conceive current reality and how we might change it? Were we created with hearts that have faith to believe in the impossible?

All these questions are laced with thoughts about God's creativity, design, and cleverness for our lives. Author and Dutch priest Henri Nouwen once said,

"Our minds are always active. We analyze, reflect, daydream, or dream. There is not a moment during the day or night when we are not thinking. You might say our thinking is 'unceasing.' Sometimes we wish that we could stop thinking for a while; that would save us from many worries, guilt feelings, and fears. Our ability to think is our greatest gift, but it is also the source of our greatest pain. Do we have to become victims of our unceasing thoughts? No, we can convert our unceasing thinking into unceasing prayer by making our inner monologue into a continuing dialogue with our God, who is the source of all love. Let's break out of our isolation and realize that Someone who dwells in the center of our beings wants to listen with love to all that occupies and preoccupies our minds."[1]

Since I am the type of person who is constantly thinking and dreaming, those words bring me great comfort and peace. My inner spirit can be the greatest gift to connect with the Lord. I truly believe God cares deeply for the affections and dreams of our hearts. He longs to become a part of everything that occupies and preoccupies our inner lives.

If not, it wouldn't make sense for him to give us the ability to envision them. Likewise, it wouldn't make sense for God to give us taste buds if he didn't have some intention for us to enjoy wine, ice cream, biscuits, chocolate, and whiskey. By its nature, the human heart has a propensity to dream. It is how we were made, a reflection of the Maker's imagination.

Yet, those dreams can often lower us into oceans of disappointment when they go unrealized. So, what are we supposed to do? How are we supposed to respond? What does it mean for our lives when our dreams are crushed and go unanswered?

In recent conversations I've had with people around this idea, I've found that I'm not alone. A similar result is felt in the human heart when a dream turns into a disappointment. There is a great tendency to become weathered, sorrowful, and frustrated with the collapse of desire.

What may be worse is when someone stops dreaming altogether. Something I'm sure we've all experienced. The pain and hurt we feel from shattered visions leave us unable to dream again. There is the onset of fear and doubt. Is it even worth having hope, dreaming again, and believing that something could change?

This is where I believe Jesus longs to meet us. As if we've got a target right on our desires for his love and care. Jesus is right there with us in the middle of our doubt and disappointment, when we don't believe anything good could ever come again. I wonder if that's exactly the type of soil our hearts need for faith to take root and flourish.

Maybe it's in those shattered dreams and torn up hopes that we need to realize God is lovingly sovereign over us. He enters into our tears, confusion, and aloneness. In those moments where hope is deferred, when our dreams come up short, Jesus is right there with us. Often, the rubble and stone of ruined dreams becomes a home base for God's redemptive work. After everything has collapsed in our lives stands one who cannot fall but chooses to come low to comfort us.

I've come to believe these moments are often the birthplace for belief. One of my favorite TV shows, Ted Lasso, talks about a phrase about not getting your hopes up. One of my favorite scenes in the show is when Ted confronts this pessimistic attitude and says, "So I've been hearing this phrase y'all got over here that I ain't too crazy about. 'It's the hope that kills you.' Y'all know that? I disagree, you know? I think it's the lack of hope that comes and gets you. See, I believe in hope. I believe in belief."[2]

It's a good thing to have hope. Just when things look bleak and unlikely to ever change is when we finally come to realize and understand that God has a much wider eye of wisdom for knowing what is good for us. Our failings and shortcomings can display our small and timid dreams. God has much brighter, deeper, and more wonderful purposes for our greatest good than we imagined. Without the death of our dreams, we wouldn't quite understand what God can do with the ashes.

We might also find that false hopes will fail us, but the dreams and hopes of heaven are weightier and more wonderful than imagined, which are worth taking up and bearing. It is in the disappointment of a washed-up dream that we might see our dreams anew through the lens of eternity. We might begin to dream again, but with more heavenly purpose and vision for what God longs to fulfill in our lives.

Dallas Willard expresses that, "Desires are terrible masters. The objects of desire may differ; I may want to eat or sleep, I may want to dominate others, I may want great wealth. Taken by themselves, desires are inherently chaotic and deceitful."[3] With that in mind, we need to be careful with how we talk about desires and dreams. Have you ever surrendered your dreams to God so he can transform them to reflect the glory of heaven?

The Psalmist asserts, "Delight yourself in the LORD and he will give you the desires of your heart" (Psalm 37:4 ESV). I used to think this meant God just wanted to give me the longings of my heart. I selfishly used to gloss over the first part of that verse and only read the second half.

Years later, with much loving correction, God has shown me that through delighting myself in him, my entire heart is transformed. By delighting myself in Jesus, my heart begins to desire things of heaven. As I satisfy myself with God, my desires begin to reflect his very heart.

As I've watched several dreams wither away over the years and sat in the absence of those hopes, I've found comfort in the words and liturgy in Every Moment Holy by Douglas McKelvy that expresses a prayer for the death of a dream. McKelvy writes:

> "So let me be tutored by this new disappointment. Let me listen to its holy whisper, that I may release at last these lesser dreams. That I might embrace the better dreams you dream for me, and for your people, and for your kingdom, and for your creation. Let me join myself to these, investing all hope in the one hope that will never come undone or betray those who place their trust in it. Teach me to hope, O Lord, always and only in you. You are the King of my collapse. You answer not what I demand, but what I do not even know what to ask. Now take this dream, this husk, this chaff of my desire, and give it back, reformed and remade according to your better vision, or do not give it back at all. Here in the ruins of my wrecked expectation, let me make this confession: Not my dreams, O Lord, not my dreams, but yours, be done. Amen."[4]

This is the surpassing life we find in the Lord. The ability to commune with the King of our collapse and discern how it can be redeemed and remade into a better, more heavenly vision. The sacred call to a life of fullness dwells in those last lines. Not our dreams, O Lord, not my dreams, but yours be done.

The ability for us to hold loosely to our dreams while trusting the God of creation to form and transform our desires to those of heaven. A crossroads of our tiny little hopes and dreams with those that have echoed and reverberated throughout the cosmos by the divine. Dreams that will most certainly, if not experienced on this side of glory, be realized and enjoyed on the other.

So go now back to those places where your disappointments rang loud in the night. Wander back to the moments where your hope was crushed thin. Take a moment to consider why your hope fell apart and how your vision faded.

Invite the God of wonder and King of dreams to do his redeeming and restoring work in your story through those hopes deferred. For you have not been abandoned. Rather, God has been burning away those dross desires and lesser longings, like impurities in gold, to bring about his goodness and glory in your life and story.

Chapter Ten

Lindsey Darling

Lindsey crashed upon me with her grace and grandeur like a wave to the shore, and my life has never been the same. She has been a conduit of joy and hope for my heart for many years. She has brought peace and rest to my weary soul during some of life's most wounding moments. Her loveliness and beauty are an ocean of wonder that always carries me back to the harbor of God's goodness and grace.

I have known who I am in Jesus more deeply and profoundly because of the way she encourages, serves, and refines this undeserving heart of mine. Lindsey is my ultimate companion, confidant, and lover. The one I will turn to at the end of this life and say, "I'm glad you are here with me. Here at the end of all things."[1]

Our lives overlapped at Rockbridge Alum Springs, a resort-quality Young Life camp in Goshen, Virginia. We were going to different colleges at the time, but it just so happened that we were volunteering to serve at camp on the same weekend. It was a whirlwind of a trip, much like the weather in late autumn that accompanied it.

I'll never forget those first moments interacting with Lindsey. I first saw her in the dining hall at camp, her hickory-brown hair and walnut-shaded eyes catching my attention from across the room. Her laughter had gravity, and the way she smiled convinced me I had never known true loveliness until then.

Over the course of the trip, I missed my share of opportunities to say hello, but God would have his way and we would briefly interact with one another at the end of the weekend. I felt like a middle school boy nervously stammering through conversation with her, just trying to keep it together. We exchanged a few words and then parted ways. I was way out of my league and completely forgot to get her name. Still, that fleeting moment would leave me daydreaming about her for months on end.

It was several days later that I found out we had mutual friends, made my move by messaging her on Facebook, and prayed to God she'd respond. Sure enough, she did, and we made plans for lunch together at James Madison University. By the grace of Jesus, I didn't totally blow our first date, and she kept me around for some time after that.

It took almost a year of me courting her until she finally gave over to my charm and we took on the title of boyfriend and girlfriend. Several lovely years later, I knew the time had come to propose and did some detective work to find a ring that would match her style. I found out that most girls had a Pinterest board secretly pinning ideas about engagements and wedding things. I felt restless with energy and excitement for this next adventure. Everything in my head and heart seemed ready to take the next step, but everything else in my story was way behind.

I had just graduated from the University of Mary Washington with a degree in economics but had struck out with finding a good job. Without having work secured before the end of senior year, I moved in with my parents for the summer after graduation to come up with a game plan. My dreams with tennis had just died as well. If I wanted to ask Lindsey for her hand in marriage, I better have more of my story ironed out. Especially those bigger life questions about how I was going to afford a place to live, provide a future, and build our lives together.

You know, questions from Lindsey that might sound like: "Hey Sean, I want to marry you and all, but are we going to be able to afford rent?" or "Honey, this all sounds wonderful, but do we have money for food next week?" I didn't need to have it all put together, but at the very least, I felt the conviction to have some sort of plan laid out. A vision I believed in and could invite Lindsey into.

I thought my first big break came with being an advisor at a financial securities firm. I snagged a couple suits, got the licensing required to practice advising, and dreamed of making a ton of money. One week later, I was fired. No kidding. After this, I went back to the drawing board and started applying at other companies.

A few bad job interviews later, and I was back to square one. My bank account was in a downward spiral. At this point in my life, buying a diamond ring was way out of the question, but my longing to marry Lindsey remained.

I wanted to figure things out, but as a hopeless romantic, everything felt incredibly overwhelming. I believed in what I wanted to pursue with Lindsey, but the road to get there was kicking my tail. My story needed to change or this whole engagement thing wasn't going to happen.

I made some well-intended phone calls to some family friends in town and eventually snagged a part-time job apprenticing at a civil engineering company. A seemingly irrelevant trajectory for a recent economics graduate, but I needed to gain some traction. Mainstream culture will tell you to always move upward, but I had just moved laterally and backwards all at the same time.

I spent that fall sitting out in fields calculating and measuring the contours of geography for that engineering firm. It wasn't glamorous, and I often sat for hours on end daydreaming about a thousand other things I'd rather be doing. But that's where God had me at the time, and that's exactly what I did. I received my first paycheck and immediately realized I had a long way to go before I'd make a dent in the engagement ring fund.

Autumn slowly passed, the air grew chilly, and winter sunsets crept further into the afternoon hours of the day. I was months away from buying a ring and popping the question. What felt like a vibrant dream on the horizon was turning into a mirage. I made the decision to settle in. To slow down. To realize that things would take much longer than I wanted and that maybe that was a good thing. Maybe God had something for me to learn on the journey to proposing.

One day, alone out in a field, God gave me this idea to craft a wooden ring box. It wouldn't be the iconic red velvet box you see in movies, but instead, it would be an artisan piece that more accurately reflects Lindsey and I's relationship. The box would be something I could put my own touch on. A vessel handcrafted from wood in my grandfather's workshop to house and contain the diamond ring.

And so that's what began to take my attention and stir my affections. It fueled and kept the engine of my life running through those colder months. I'd get home from being out in the field and head straight to the workshop.

I found some old pieces of oak, walnut, and maple that Eugene had in his shop and began to carve the wood. I wasn't working on something grand or excessive, but this little box commanded so much of my attention and creativity. I ended up making it four different times because it needed to be just right. The sanding, shaping, and staining finally culminated into a piece of craftsmanship that I was proud of. It was an engagement ring box I had completely invested myself into making which would one day hold the stone and symbol of my commitment to Lindsey.

Most of it seemed like fiddling at times, but in retrospect, that season of my story brought me substantial life experiences. During a time in my life when I really didn't have much working out for me, God was working. When I felt like I was hitting a dead end, God was making a way. God was taking me through his school of sanctification. He was teaching me to be an artisan of life. He was teaching me the purpose of investing myself into a worthy cause.

It wasn't just on this material level, but it was on a heart level. I began to realize I had the opportunity to craft my story. I had the ability to align myself with God's intentions for my life through creativity and artistry. It was in those cold nights in the workshop with stained hands that I realized God has entrusted us with great imagination and purpose to craft our own lives.

Our stories can be mended and molded to reflect the one true story God is sharing with the world. This discovery helped me understand the purpose and significance to the activities of my life. It allowed me to view each moment of my day as an act of creativity and expression. It added immense value to the trivial times of life, which when added up, become a much greater tapestry telling the wonderful story of God.

In his book The Artisan Soul, Erwin McManus writes, "To create is to reflect the image of God. To create is an act of worship…If your greatest work of art is the life you live, and ultimately life is a creative act, what life will you choose to leave behind as your masterpiece?"[2] This is the question we are faced with every single day of our lives.

If we've been given the imagination and creativity of heaven, what story are we going to tell? What are we creating with our lives? What is your story telling the world around it? From this angle, life becomes so much more about artistry and beauty.

To craft a remarkable life is to embody the Creator himself. Creating and shaping a life beyond measure is an act and expression of worship. We get to experience the wholeness of life by worshiping God in our creativity. As we live and shape our lives through our thoughts, motives, and actions we step into avenues of experiencing God's very heart for our stories.

My time in the workshop continued, the holidays passed, a new year started, and winter dragged on. The cold brisk air turned feathery and light as spring drew near. Life began to buzz and rebirth around me. The weight of the engagement ring had burned with anticipation against my heart for months now. The box was finished, and the diamond ring sat perched within. The moment had come for a young boy's longing to become reality.

I took Lindsey back to where our lives first brushed up against each other at Rockbridge. I had some modest plans arranged by convincing my friend Landon to hide in the woods to photograph the big moment. Lindsey and I made our way into the cross hairs of his camera lens, and I knelt on my knee. I'll be honest: I don't remember what was said, but I do recall the life altering "yes" that affirmed our lives together. We were set on a trajectory into the wondrous adventure of marriage.

Several months passed, wedding plans were ironed out, and the big day arrived with forecasts of rain. Not exactly the weather you're hoping for on your wedding day outside on a farm in the middle of June. We shrugged our shoulders, said a prayer, and pressed on, half-convinced we would be standing in puddles saying our vows. Sometimes you just have to be content with what's ahead of you, hold onto one another, and enjoy the adventure.

Not a single drop of rain hit the ground that afternoon, but there was plenty of wind. Our friend and pastor David, who officiated the wedding, spoke off script of the significance of wind in scripture and turned our attention to the Holy Spirit, who is often associated with the wind. He reminded us that God was blowing life, love, and goodness upon our lives.

I look back on those early days with Lindsey and realize we're still the same playful kids at the altar. We just have a little more wisdom and insight about life and relationships now. We've journeyed farther into life since that windy day on Sunny Slope Farm. We've grown in our understanding of God's deep love for us and how it should overflow into our marriage.

We're gentler and kinder with one another. We wake up every single day, regardless of feelings, and we say "yes" again and again to each other. We say "yes" to whatever comes our way for better or worse. We strain forward together, trusting Jesus has a purpose for our stories. We approach life as an adventure and opportunity to craft our stories alongside God.

This has stuck with me for years. This is the doorway to walking deeply with Jesus. It's seeing and seizing the ability to craft your life with him. You and I are given the opportunity to create a life of fullness alongside the God of the universe. We get to take whatever our lives may look like, surrender them over to God, and then, as an artisan, turn them into a work of art. Whatever life may look like, Jesus has laid out a redemptive and providential path for your story.

So, let's craft our lives to point to heaven. Let's use our stories to make the kingdom of Jesus more tangible. Be the most kingdom-minded teacher you can be. The most Christ-centered nurse, lawyer, janitor, chef, stay-at-home mom, or inventor possible. Be the greatest reflection of Jesus to a world that is desperate for good news.

Point your heart towards Christ as you live out your life. Becoming the best father, mother, husband, wife, brother, sister, friend, or neighbor you can be. Filtering your life through the gospel. Commit to the flourishing of the world around you through gospel-centered living. Whatever your story includes, craft every part of it to imitate the heart of God. This is the journey into a life that overflows with wonder and goodness.

When we moved into our house a few years ago, I found the old wooden ring box tucked away in moving containers with some other keepsakes. I hadn't laid eyes on it for years and completely forgot the different contours of the wood. I noticed the different grain and texture of the formed pieces. I gazed at the various stains and hues of oak, walnut, and maple. It was imperfect, yet wonderfully captured my heart for Lindsey all those years ago.

I couldn't help but stand there and weep thinking about everything in life that has unfolded over the years. So much has changed since we committed our lives to each other, but the central part of our hearts remains true, and the ring box is symbolic of that. Almost more significantly, it's a reflection of Jesus, the first lover of our hearts, as he woos us into an exceedingly deep life with him. Our response to that invitation will make all the difference.

Chapter Eleven
Venom and Vince Guaraldi

The trees have turned gold in the hills, and the autumn air grows crisp and cold. All the green from summer is fading, and in one last flourish, everything has turned amber, crimson, and maroon. Our first fire of the year burns warm in the wood stove and invites me to rest and linger.

Life is starting to slow down out of reverence to nature's decay outside my window. It is finally time to catch my breath. My Vince Guaraldi vinyl crackles on the record player with sounds of "A Charlie Brown Christmas." It's the most wonderful time of the year, and for our family, that means quite a few traditions.

One of my favorite traditions is to pile into the family car, drive out into the Blue Ridge mountains, cut down a Christmas tree, and haul it back home. It's a time for wearing warm festive outfits, sipping hot chocolate, and listening to Christmas classics like Bing Crosby and Frank Sinatra. We fuel nostalgia with fondness, music, laughter, and cheer. There's a tree farm we've been visiting for years in Southwest Virginia where you can walk for miles through thickly lined rows of Frasier firs. It usually takes us several hours to find the perfect one to haul home, but it's always filled with discovery.

Years ago, for our first married Christmas together, Lindsey and I wanted to carry on the tradition. We lived in Charlotte, North Carolina and would be traveling to Virginia for the holidays, so we planned to bring back a tree for ourselves. The only catch we ran into was transporting it back to our little apartment on Bonita Lane.

You should've seen us in our compact Toyota Corolla with this eight-foot tree draped over the top. It looked like a scene out of National Lampoon's Christmas Vacation. You wouldn't have thought there'd be any pine left on the tree after we drove it down the interstate, but sure enough, we made it home with plenty of needles left on its limbs, threw it in a stand, and started decorating.

Once it was adorned with lights, bows, ornaments, and ribbons, it was quite heavenly and smelled lovely. There's something innately magical about a Christmas tree illuminating a room with its rays and aromas. Christmastime has a way of lighting up people like bulbs on a tree.

After several weeks of having the tree up and decorated inside our apartment, I received a frantic call from Lindsey one afternoon. Through loss of breath, she stuttered through the phone that there was a snake wrapping itself around an ornament. I was absolutely lost for words. Lindsey on the other end of the phone was frozen in place, standing in the kitchen, staring across the room into the eyes of a living, breathing snake.

All sorts of terrifying fears hit me at once. We had been within inches of that tree countless times over the past weeks. Eating meals, napping, and hanging with friends. How close had one of us come to the snake and not realized it? Did it come out and make its way onto the couch occasionally? What did it do while we were sleeping?

I was shocked and literally had no clue what to do or how to help on the other end of the phone. Unfortunately, it hid itself back inside the branches before we could get to it. We had no clue what to do. Should we just throw the tree out and let this snake-sized-Grinch steal our Christmas spirit? Would we feel comfortable at all just leaving the tree up knowing this little monster was lurking inside?

In one last effort, with the help of some friends, we stripped the entire tree of decorations, took it outside, and combed through it to see what we could find. We looked branch by branch for a couple hours but found nothing. We had a big dilemma on our hands. Do we throw out the tree we had invested hours in or just put it back up, hoping the snake had been ditched in the process?

I'm sure you've already made your own decision of what you would've done in our shoes. I'm guessing most people would've gone with the first option, and I don't blame you. We took the second. I know it was risky, but we had invested so much time and effort into this tree, the tradition, and experience that we weren't going to let something like this take it away. I admit we didn't sleep well the first week, but time passed, and we went on to celebrate Christmas and the New Year without any other snake sightings. We kept the tree up until it eventually lost all its needles by February. I admit, we're those crazy people who go all out for the holidays, but don't judge us, we just really love that time of year.

It sounds crazy, but I learned a lot from our snake tree and the chaos it created in our lives for a couple weeks. I think our stories are a lot like Christmas trees, or at least they can be. They have the capacity to light up a room and bring hope, joy, and wonder to the people around us.

You and I can decorate our lives to be magical, even in the simplest of times. I'm not talking about buying more things or wearing certain clothes. I'm saying that we can array ourselves with love, joy, and peace—the fruits of the spirit—to bring life to those around us. The unfortunate reality is there are going to be things at times that creep in to steal, kill, and destroy our lives. There are going to be moments and happenings that try to snuff out the brilliance and splendor of our stories.

Scripture says we are the pleasing aroma of Christ. Essentially this sweet, captivating fragrance that pleases God and draws people to him. Just like the scent of evergreen and pine can enchant our senses during the holidays. Without a doubt, the way we live our stories has a lot of gravity on those around us. The way we invest our time, how we treat others, and who we become can illuminate the heart of Jesus. Our stories can have the allure to point people to the goodness and beauty of God the same way a Christmas tree lights up a child's eyes in December with wonder.

The challenge in our stories comes from things trying to sabotage our faith. Without a doubt we will experience resistance when trying to live life alongside Jesus. Hardship and trials can beat us to a pulp. Fear can take the driver seat at times and derail our stories. There are moments when we may want to ditch our faith altogether because it's lost its luster, just like we wanted to toss the Christmas tree out the front door.

Faith's sparkle and splendor can be zapped from us in an instant because of fearfulness and worry. Our job is to look past it all and lock eyes on Jesus. Bob Goff says, "Courage isn't the absence of fear; it's just deciding that fear isn't calling the shots anymore."[1] I love that thought. If our lives operate most freely and profoundly when we don't let fear call the shots, then we need to hold tightly to courage and hope.

It's no wonder that the phrase "do not fear" shows up more than three hundred times in Scripture. When we give ourselves over to fear, we give it the power to dictate our lives. This is why God commands, "So do not fear, for I am with you; do not be dismayed, for I am your God. I will strengthen you and help you; I will uphold you with my righteous right hand" (Isaiah 41:10 NIV).

Living out this verse in Isaiah doesn't come easy though. Especially when you're crying in your car after receiving a bad diagnosis or after getting the call of a loved one's death. Life can be absolutely brutal and make hope feel like a lost cause.

Experiencing hardship is the reality of a fallen world. Jesus even said to his disciples, "I have told you these things, so that in me you may have peace. In this world you will have trouble. But take heart! I have overcome the world." (John 16:33 NIV). Jesus didn't shy away from a hard life himself. He lived and walked this earth and encountered terrible things. If life didn't hold back on the savior, what makes us think it'll be easier on us? The sooner we realize we can be wounded by a world ready to deal a devastating blow, the more we'll recognize our need for Jesus.

I think it's also worth noting that following Jesus isn't an easy road, but it's the most worthwhile endeavor we can pursue with our lives. It will cost us everything—be sure of that—but we will gain heaven in return. Jesus in a conversation with his friends said, "For whoever wants to save their life will lose it, but whoever loses their life for me and for the gospel will save it. What good is it for someone to gain the whole world, yet forfeit their soul?" (Mark 8:35-36 NIV). This is the way of a remarkable life, which is radically different from what the world will try to sell you, but it's the gosh darn truth. We will find our lives when we push aside our fears and selfishness.

Dying to self is not a glamorous experience, but it's the pathway to discovering the wholesome life Jesus offers. Following Jesus is a journey of denying ourselves in order to truly live. God doesn't exist to scold us and hold out on us. His desire isn't to perpetually decline and reject our pleasure.

Instead, God's longing is to give us long lasting joy. This is why David in the Psalms expresses, "The lines have fallen for me in pleasant places; indeed, I have a beautiful inheritance. I bless the LORD who gives me counsel; in the night also my heart instructs me. I have set the LORD always before me; because he is at my right hand, I shall not be shaken" (Psalm 16:6-8 NIV). David understands that God isn't some begrudging King who denies his people pleasure and goodness. The Psalmist understands that God gives man and woman boundaries for their own good. A framework that is pleasant and leads to human flourishing.

This is the heart of God, and this is why he has defined, in his own words, specific ways for us to live our lives. As Christians, we have different ethics than the rest of the world for a reason. It's because God established the healthy and right way for humans to live. The heart of God is for his people to find joy and flourish. His instructions and encouragement for our lives isn't to withhold anything, but rather to lead us into goodness.

This is true for all facets of life. God has a design for how we approach and treat money. He has instructions for relationships, work, rest, sex, and recreation. The list goes on, but the notion is the same. God's heart is to bring us an abundance of life through himself and his creation. When we live outside of God's design, good things become destructive tendencies.

So, as we consider God's design for life, let us not forget the healthy boundaries that God has set before us. As we grow within this framework, we understand that pursuing Jesus is costly, yet leads to abundant life. We could choose so many different people from the Bible as examples for this.

Paul, for example, was set on following Jesus. He had massive hopes and dreams for sharing the gospel with many different people and nations throughout the world. His heart was pointed toward God, and where did it take him? It ended up leading him into jail cells, shipwrecks, deserted islands, perilous cities, persecution, and beatings. None of that sounds like the way we'd draw it up, but that's the way God often works. He uses fear, setbacks, and weakness to draw us to himself. Let's not forget that Paul was the one who penned, "That is why, for Christ's sake, I delight in weaknesses, in insults, in hardships, in persecutions, in difficulties. For when I am weak, then I am strong" (2 Corinthians 12:10 NIV).

When I started telling our friends we put the tree back up, they thought we were crazy. Honestly, they were right. We were foolishly hopeful, a trait that often resides at the heart of following Jesus. Lindsey and I had no clue if the snake was still in the tree, but we were holding onto hope.

We weren't going to let the snake, a symbol of fear and resistance, steal Christmas from us. The tree represented so much more to us than just some ornately decorated pine. It reflected the whole experience of our stories and the things that try to steal and kill the joy in our lives.

The heartbreaking reality is that we view our stories as that beat-up Frasier fir laying outside on the curb. Things have come into our lives like that sly snake and hijacked our wonder and delight. Experiences, hardship, and setbacks have sucked the faith out of us and laid waste to our longings and hopes.

Circumstances have pressured us to hit eject on our spirituality and doubt the goodness of God. We're wading in the ripples of a fallen world. We're bruised and battered. Maybe even tired of following Jesus at times, but that's exactly where he wants to reclaim our stories.

Jesus wants to use you, your gifts, and your longings to bring his kingdom into people's lives. He wants to use your story to draw people to his wooden cross and empty tomb. The hard but glorious endeavor is stepping into courage and stomping over fear. There may be plenty of setbacks, obstacles, and afflictions that grieve us along the way, but even God uses those awful and terrible happenings for our good and his glory.

The key to a life overflowing with joy is found in bravely following Jesus, trusting the boundaries he's set, and delighting in his goodness. We must hold onto hope. We have to hold onto Jesus. It is the only way our stories will come alive and alight—like a tree on Christmas morning.

Chapter Twelve

The Cadence of Christ

A few years ago, I was completely burned out and exhausted. I was living my life full throttle, and if I eventually didn't slow down, I might have crumbled under the weight of it all. I was several years into being self-employed and essentially running my own business, which was incredibly taxing. Being the boss implies you wear all the hats, but it also means you're on the hook for everything.

We had also just welcomed our oldest daughter Evelyn into the world, which was simultaneously wonderful and tiresome. We were committing to a lot of things. Life felt rushed and chaotic. Hurrying from one event to another at a constantly hustled pace, Lindsey and I really started to experience the consequence of a life without boundaries.

Even when I did slow down, my attention was distracted and divided. My ability to connect and engage with family, friends, and neighbors felt fractured. I was desperately in need of a life that placed more emphasis on rest and rhythm.

Don't get me wrong. I enjoyed experiencing the growth I was having with work, I cherished every moment of our young, flourishing family, and I enjoyed saying "yes" to people and feeling like I was someone people could rely on. But soon enough, it all became unhealthy, and I started to justify my overload as the new normal.

I masqueraded everything as heroism, grit, and guts, but inside, I was wearing away. The hurried lifestyle we had wrapped ourselves around was exhausting. I often woke up in the middle of the night consumed with anxiety. My mind was constantly racing, and the erosion of progress was setting in. I felt the pressure and restlessness of a culture that never slowed down.

One night, I remember stumbling downstairs in the middle of winter and fumbling for Every Moment Holy. I flipped through the worn-out bindings to page 95—a page I had become familiar with. This specific prayer was titled "For Those Who Cannot Sleep." I found myself reciting the prayer through sobs of lament laced with anger.

I forced, bitterly, my prayers toward God. On the outside, I looked like a relatively successful man with a vibrant marriage, robust career, and happy family. But the outside world knew nothing of my internal struggle and distress. I laid on the floor in tears, unable to fall back asleep, praying that God would meet me in my pain. I desperately needed the good shepherd to lead me by green pastures and still waters. My heart ached to be still.

After several hours alone in the dark, I sensed Jesus opening my heart to his gentle spirit. His subtle nudge turned my attention to the state of my story. I started to take inventory of the way I had been living and realized I was going about it all wrong. My priorities, while they may have been sincere, were way out of order. I had neglected the rhythm and rest my life desperately needed.

It dawned on me that for months, God had been trying to slow me down. To show me that as Christians, our lives are designed to have a unique tempo and cadence. We are created to be still. Jesus invites us into this way of living when he asserts, "Come to me, all you who are weary and burdened, and I will give you rest. Take my yoke upon you and learn from me, for I am gentle and humble in heart, and you will find rest for your souls. For my yoke is easy and my burden is light" (Matthew 11:28-30 NIV). Jesus is inviting us into a story where rest is the main cadence. Rest that is plentiful, appropriate, healthy for our lives.

There is a unique way in which we as followers of Jesus can live. Dane Ortlund in Gentle and Lowly writes; "You don't need to unburden or collect yourself and then come to Jesus. Your very burden is what qualifies you to come. No payment is required; he says, 'I will give you rest.' His rest is gift, not transaction. Whether you are actively working hard to crowbar your life into smoothness ('labor') or passively finding yourself weighed down by something outside your control ('heavy laden'), Jesus Christ's desire that you find rest, that you come in out of the storm, outstrips even your own.".[1] There is a way for our stories to embody the rest Jesus is talking about. There is a channel for living that integrates a healthy rhythm of rest in our daily activities and responsibilities.

This idea of yoke may not make much sense to us in the western world since most of us aren't farmers or ranchers. But, to someone in the first century, the term yoke would have been completely relatable. When Jesus talks about a yoke, he is referring to the heavy bar laid on oxen, which enables them to do their job of pulling equipment needed for farming. What Jesus is sharing here is that we can learn from him. We can take his yoke upon us, which enables us to find rest in him while stewarding our daily chores and responsibilities. Taking Christ's yoke upon us frees us from the very burdens that overwhelm us.

In that burned-out season of my life, I certainly didn't want to take on anything new or add something else to my to-do list. But that's the wonderful thing about leaning into Jesus. Taking his yoke upon us does not add more pressure and stress to our lives. Instead, it is a posture, awareness, and confession of our hearts. Taking the yoke of Jesus adjusts and reforms our stories.

Jesus himself says that his yoke is easy, and his burden is light—how could it be anything else? Dane Ortlund also writes: "Jesus is using a kind of irony, saying that the yoke laid on his disciples is a nonyoke. For it is a yoke of kindness. Who could resist this? It's like telling a drowning man that he must put on the burden of a life preserver only to hear him shout back, sputtering, "No way! Not me! This is hard enough, drowning here in these stormy waters. The last thing I need is the added burden of a life preserver around my body!"[2] This is the posture of the heart for the person who has received the yoke of Christ. The paradox of God's yoke and burden is that it brings rest and rhythm to our stories.

Leaning into the ways of Jesus leads us into a heavenly cadence of shalom, the profound psychological and emotional peace of God, that edifies our souls. Taking up the yoke of Jesus is not about crowbarring our stories into submission, but rather relying on Jesus for rest and rejuvenation. He is the way, the truth, and the life. Coming under his yoke and walking his path will inject repose and peace into our stories.

It realigns our lives and brings us into a position where we're able to live more wholly and function more acutely in the Spirit. It bleeds into our daily lives as we begin to uncover God's design for how we can truly find rest and rhythm. It is understanding that God has an intended design for how we spend our time. It is establishing a cadence of connecting with God in the mundanity.

The opposite of this comes through the busyness and noise our culture constantly bolsters. Getting caught in the tow and tumble of constant activity almost happens effortlessly. The constant portrayal of being busy is almost becoming a normal way of living. Life keeps chugging along until the "check engine" light comes on and we realize we're burned out. We find ourselves, like Bilbo Baggins in the Lord of the Rings saying, "I feel thin, sort of stretched, like butter scraped over too much bread."[3]

The world is enamored with the never-ending hustle and bustle. It constantly promotes acceleration, growth, and attainment. Our society is addictive, and we latch onto the drug. How many times in conversations at work, around the neighborhood, or with friends do you hear people answer how they're doing with "I've been busy?"

Honestly, I do it all the time because it's true, and I feel a sense of pride when saying it. But it's absolutely killing me. When did being busy become one of the major identifiers for our stories? Does anyone want to be remembered for being busy? But this is how most of us live our lives. We're living in a constant state of weariness perpetuated by busyness.

In the U.S. sitcom The Office, one of the characters (Andy Bernard) spins the phrase, "I wish there was a way to know you were in the good old days before you actually left them."[4] This is exactly the way most people live their lives. Unaware of the goodness, wonder, and sanctity of life because of how distracting the everyday urgency becomes. We don't understand the harm our constant activity and movement is causing to our hearts.

Few of us know how to truly rest anymore, and with lifestyles that turn so quickly from one thing to the next, we half-heartedly believe we can slow down. We're absorbed with things clamoring for our attention and affection. Our constant coming and going has left us exhausted. We continue to bear the yoke of a distracted culture desperate for relief.

No wonder most of us are worn out and overwhelmed by everything. Our constant activity has blinded us to the daily beauty around us. Establishing a cadence of rest is crucial to the longevity and stamina of our souls. There's no surprise our world is plagued with fatigue when we've neglected the fundamental need we have for rest and shalom.

When I speak about rest and rhythm, I'm talking about creating the space for our hearts to breathe and realign with God. We are finite creatures that have limited capacities. Our connection with God is how we develop resilience in an overworked and overscheduled culture. Removing the noise and making space for our souls to breathe.

Our biological makeup is designed to decompress from a world that is overexerted. Remember, God's yoke is kindness and freedom from stress, strain, and struggle. True rest is a process of turning everything and everyone over to God, releasing the tensions of a fallen world and finding peace in Jesus. This doesn't mean we won't experience stress and strain in our lives, but coming to Jesus is the antidote against those very pressures. Resting and reuniting with him daily is the avenue to a faithful life.

Finding rest in Christ is not about catching up on sleep (although that may be important), but rather a soulful connection and resetting with God. Although resting in the Lord may be physical, it is much more about communing and connecting with Jesus. One can enter God's rest while praying on an afternoon run. One may enter rest while reading a book that provokes the heart toward Christ.

Union with God may be diverse. Finding rest in him can look different for each person. It could be going on a hike, watching a sunset, listening to jazz music, or enjoying the fondness of friends and a good meal. It will also include disciplines like prayer, fasting, and reading Scripture. I think there are many ways to engage the Lord and receive his love and restfulness. The pivotal point is that we start somewhere.

Finding rest is all encompassing. If our heart is the culmination of who we are and the controlling piece of what leads and guides us, then when our hearts are depleted, we will have nothing to offer the world. This is the importance of the human heart finding rest and union with Jesus.

He is calling us out of our hurried and exhausted state into his gentleness and rest. The author of Hebrews writes, "Let us, therefore, make every effort to enter that rest, so that no one will perish by following their example of disobedience" (Hebrews 4:11 NIV). Here it is, right before us, the opportunity to drop from our lives the concerns which so easily trouble us. In redirecting our lives to the fountain of living water, we will truly experience repose.

After that revelation of rest hit me, laying on my living room floor, I made the commitment to adjust my life accordingly. I decided to take Wednesdays off from then on. It was an act against the grain. A non-negotiable day. A decision to rediscover my hardwiring and find time with Jesus and my family.

It was a counterattack against the assault I felt from my environment saying work harder and longer and throw your life aside. It felt wildly self-destructive at the time. I questioned myself and what God was calling me into. I heard the lies of the enemy creeping in, "Sean, you're self-employed! If you don't work, you'll go poor," "Taking a day off is destructive to your business," and "This is going to ruin you!" But the call from God was pressed upon my story, so I leaned even further into Wednesdays as a sabbath for our family.

Committing to this habit on Wednesdays and creating the space to rest and connect with God has made all the difference in my story. It makes room for me to pull my head out of the trenches to truly grasp what's going on in my life. Not every Wednesday looks the same. Most of these days are mundane, but they're filled with what I would call the deeper things in life. Time with my family, friends, and Jesus. Time to be still, think, pray, and reflect on what God is doing in me. It's space to grow, learn, read, and write. Moments to engage the heart of Jesus in ways I'm created for.

I know most people won't have the ability to just take off during the middle of the week. Being my own boss has its advantages at times, but regardless, finding rest and communing with God is central to the Christian life. Despite your calendar, start creating margin for silence and solitude with God.

Turn over your busyness to Jesus and fight for time with him. It could be setting your alarm earlier than usual to start your day with God. You may need to carve out time during the day to take inventory of how your soul is doing. Maybe it's using your lunch break to sit and pray.

The Christian life is not just believing in Jesus, but following his lifestyle, and following Jesus is practicing and forming habits that reflect the way he lives. Sometimes, it's inconvenient, it disrupts our lives (and others'), and many times, it's countercultural. But Jesus lived an unhurried life on purpose.

John Mark Comer writes, "The solution to an overbusy life is not more time. It's to slow down and simplify our lives around what really matters."[6] Jesus was the type of person who lived with great intention and pace but was never rushed. The cadence of Christ is a heavenly tempo of rest.

Jesus was not a sluggish human living aimlessly, but rather an individual with deep propensity for purpose and measure. Jesus lived with a meaningful rhythm to his life. He was tuned into his heart and life with his father. Jesus was able to properly connect with people because he had established a rhythm of rest.

We must eliminate hurriedness from our lives. A way of living that dilutes the sacred things of life and prevents us from being present in the moment. It's been years now, but I still take Wednesdays off, which has reminded me that the sabbath was made for man, not man for the sabbath.

An unhurried story is the best kind of story. Slowing down allows us to take in more of the good things in life. Being unhurried with God reinforces the way we've been designed to live. To be still, breathe, and create margin to connect with the divine. Jesus lovingly invites us into his presence where we'll find surpassing rest for our souls.

Chapter Thirteen

Parkwood

We bought our house in Richmond several years ago on New Year's Eve. We were supposed to close on the home and pick up the keys at the beginning of December, but things were delayed because of some legal hurdles. We signed the paperwork in the morning, grabbed a celebratory Chick-fil-A milkshake in the afternoon, and then made our way over to the house for our own version of demo-day. We were behind schedule with our renovation plans, so we spent the rest of the afternoon tearing apart the kitchen before heading to a New Year's Eve party.

The house is an all-brick row home built in the 1920s. The covered porch wraps across the front. Hydrangea, marigolds, snap dragons, and phlox grow in the front flower beds. The wrought iron door sways on its hundred-year-old hinges. It is a captivating and beautiful place filled with wonder, character, and charm. When we bought it, you could tell it held memories and showed its age. Yet there was a longing that echoed within its walls to be restored. It had secrets hidden away that ached to be discovered. This house was quite the talker, creaking and moaning from its glory days.

For years Lindsey and I wanted to have our own home, but more than that, we wanted the opportunity to take something worn out and restore it to its former splendor. For several years before this, we had been renting a small apartment a few blocks over. We would bike up and down Richmond's cobblestone streets with faint dreams and hopes that one day, we might just own one of the houses we rode by.

A place we could renew and put our own touch on. It was a hopeful but fainthearted prayer, and I mostly doubted it would ever come true. We would learn years later that God had put that longing in us and was bringing it to fruition.

Our biggest dilemma was that we couldn't afford to purchase the house and cover the renovation work it desperately needed. Either the work would have to wait until we saved up enough money to hire professionals, or we would have to take the construction into our own hands. We felt stuck.

Fortunately, I had spent several summers during high school and college doing construction work with my father. He took on some home renovation projects for a few friends while I was growing up and hired me to work alongside him. There were a few homes that we finished and reconditioned over the years together that gave me knowledge and familiarity with the construction world.

I learned a ton apprenticing with him and knew I could lean on him if we committed to the work. This gave Lindsey and I comfort as we were debating whether to take on renovating the entire house. Just knowing we would have people like my dad to lean on gave us assurance we could pull it off. Often in life, when things feel incredibly foolish and daunting, just hearing someone in your corner say "we'll figure it out" is the most comforting words imaginable. So, we went for it.

It took us six months of working nonstop before we could move in. When I say "we," I'm speaking of the tribe of family and friends who give us their time, energy, and effort during the process. As much as I had learned as an apprentice under my father, I quickly realized we couldn't sustain the house renovations alone. We needed more brains and bronze.

Lindsey and I were in over our heads and leaning on our support people would be the only way to truly revive our home. For months, our families would come stay in our little two-bedroom apartment, wake up early with us, and head over to Parkwood. Friends would join us along the way. Neighbors would chip in.

We spent the first part of winter tearing the house down to the studs and cleaning it out before we started the rebuilding process. It was cold and dark those first few weeks because we were literally redoing everything. We didn't have electricity or running water, which made the house feel empty and worn. Slowly, anticipation filled the air. Shadows began to shorten as February turned to March and spring made her way toward us. Parkwood began to rouse from its slumber while the days grew warmer. The outside world began to buzz with new life. The project really started to take shape.

What an adventure we were on! One that was both exhilarating and exhausting. Isn't that how most adventures tend to go? They're filled with all sorts of experiences and unknowns. They're loaded with things imaginable and sometimes unimaginable. They're full of all sorts of setbacks and perils. I love Samwise Gamgee's brutal honesty about the elements of story and adventure when he says in the Lord of the Rings,

> "It's like in the great stories, Mr. Frodo. The ones that really mattered. Full of darkness and danger they were. And sometimes you didn't want to know the end. Because how could the end be happy? How could the world go back to the way it was when so much bad had happened? But in the end, it's only a passing thing, this shadow. Even darkness must pass. A new day will come. And when the sun shines it will shine out the clearer. Those were the stories that stayed with you. That meant something, even if you were too small to understand why. But I think, Mr. Frodo, I do understand. I know now. Folk in those stories had lots of chances of turning back, only they didn't. They kept going, because they were holding on to something. That there is some good in this world, and it's worth fighting for."[1]

Adventures and good stories tend to engage every facet of our lives. They invoke deep emotions and affections. True adventure is filled with uncertainty, risk, and mystery. It employs all our soul, where joy, hope, and heartache clash along the way. I've come to learn that adventure is the road to an incredible life filled with meaning and fulfillment.

Although our long and strenuous work on Parkwood wasn't a matter of life and death, it still had the elements of a wonderful adventure. We finished the bulk of the project in the middle of summer and moved in. Most of our belongings sat in boxes scattered on the living room floor.

I remember being so surprised at how far we had come. Our hands hurt, our minds were spent, but our hearts were full. We accomplished more than we ever thought was possible. We renewed our old brick house while redefining ourselves along the way. The house had completely changed, and we had transformed with it.

In hindsight, our adventure with Parkwood taught me so much about life. It's hard to say which moments shaped me the most, but one vital lesson that I learned along the way is that there is richness in renewal. Our 1920s row-house was new and beautiful when it was first constructed, but over time its vibrance waned. Our house became neglected and in desperate need of restoration—and so it is with life itself. Over the years our stories can become neglected, where only an act of God can restore them to their original intent. Our lives can become so weathered and worn-out by this broken world that we are in desperate need of renewal on a heart-level.

What happened? Shouldn't life be beautiful and grand, but instead it often becomes bent and aimless? What went wrong? All we have to do is look around to see how fraudulent and uneasy life can be. Each of us could list a hundred ways we've experienced the wear and tear of life. This ache in our hearts and the unsettling things about life are all consequences of the fall. We are prone to wander, as the hymn goes.

When we start to pay close attention to the state of our hearts, we'll begin to see just how misaligned things have become. We'll start to realize how anxious and twisted our inner life can be at times. It makes sense why life can be so cruel when you multiply the reality of sin by every single person on earth. No wonder our world is hurting and we long for things to be made right.

I once heard Erwin McManus share a story about a soldier who had lost an arm but continued to feel pain as if the missing limb still existed. Erwin was explaining the idea of phantom pain, the fundamental theory that a person can ache for something they once had long after it's been lost. Human morals and truth are the phantom pain of the soul.

The reason your gut tells you things are wrong in life is because it's falling short of human standards. The phrase for this is "inhumane." It is living below the correct measure of personhood. McManus goes on to say that when a lion devours its prey, we don't say it's being in-animal or un-lion because the lion is doing exactly what we expect of predators. But when a murderer takes an innocent person's life, we label it as inhumane because it is acting against the nature of being human.

Rightly so, whenever we experience other acts of injustice, brokenness, cruelty, or malice, they are also signs of phantom pain in the soul. Our brokenness is an indication that something is missing. That something went wrong. The Christian explanation for this is sin, the ultimate loss of union with God. The result of this fractured relationship is a wounded world pleading to be rescued and restored.

The wonderful reality for our lost and damaged condition is that God planned all along to redeem and renew all things to himself. Scripture tells us of God's magnificent intention to make all things new. The disciple John recorded this revelation from Jesus,

> "And I heard a loud voice from the throne saying, 'Look! God's dwelling place is now among the people, and he will dwell with them. They will be his people, and God himself will be with them and be their God. "He will wipe every tear from their eyes. There will be no more death" or mourning or crying or pain, for the old order of things has passed away.' He who was seated on the throne said, 'I am making everything new!' Then he said, 'Write this down, for these words are trustworthy and true'"
>
> (Revelation 21:3-5 NIV)

I'm so thankful John recorded this promise from God for us to hold onto like an anchor in the storm. The audacious love of

Jesus is what drives God to restore what is ruined. Through the work of Jesus, all things are being made new. Through him, we are made right with God.

The Apostle Paul in Romans wrote, "But the gift is not like the trespass. For if the many died by the trespass of the one man, how much more did God's grace and the gift that came by the grace of the one man, Jesus Christ, overflow to the many!" (Romans 5:15 NIV). What occurred in Adam and transferred to us is now corrected through the grace of Christ. It is a wonder of wonders to see someone come to salvation in Jesus. To see a lost prodigal welcomed back into the family of God. But what does the transformed saint now do with their changed heart? How does the redeemed believer step back into a warped world?

Paul once again gives hint to this by saying, "For we are God's handiwork, created in Christ Jesus to do good works, which God prepared in advance for us to do" (Ephesians 2:10 NIV). The reformed saint is now an agent of change in God's Kingdom. The born-again Christian now dons the robe and ring of Jesus. Our identity is restored, and we are invited into mending and renewing the world.

Once we experience the newness of Jesus ourselves, we can better understand the work of redemption in the people around us. It becomes our reflex to take light into a dark world even while brokenness still exists, people are still hurting, injustice is being done, evil is at work, and disheartening events are unfolding in our stories. Part of our role to play in the coming Kingdom is pushing back against darkness.

God is light. As we work by and through his strength, we participate in the renewal of the world. We take part in witnessing lifeless people come alive. Paul uses the phrase "know in part" when he talks about the workings of God in this world. This expression tells us we may only partially understand stuff in our stories. There are many things we won't know until we stand with God face-to-face, and even then, it may not be a thought in our minds.

Later in The Lord of the Rings, Frodo says to Sam at the end of their adventures together, "You will be healed. You were meant to be solid and whole, and you will be."[3] Tolkien must've reflected this Christian idea of renewal into his writings because it reflects the workings heaven. Even Jesus himself looked at the sick, broken, and burdened people in Scripture and asked, "Do you want to be well? (John 5:6)"

This is the tug we feel in our lives and the space we can step into as we live out our stories. We are invited to be instruments, God's handiwork, in the here and now. Our lives and stories are the avenues of the coming Kingdom. Jesus is inviting us to step into each day with the assurance that God has justified us by grace through faith. And thus, we begin the journey of bringing about his renewal in our neighborhoods, workplaces, churches, families, and homes.

The mending of humanity rides in the wake of our love and goodness. A myriad of actions, deeds, prayers, and petitions. This renewal flows from simple, yet profoundly sacred moments in life.

Something as ordinary as sitting with a friend who just lost a loved one. Taking a meal to friends who welcomed a newborn. It's being there at the hospital and sharing in someone's grief. Crying with a friend who is suffering from depression and anxiety. Raising a family. Caretaking of those who are disabled. Being the coworker who doesn't jump into conversations of slander and gossip. All acts of grace and goodness carry renewal into our stories. Those mundane and commonplace happenings bear the image of the heavenly.

Regardless of our circumstances, let us strive to treat each day with the confidence that God is working and moving amongst us with love and grace. He has promised to work for the good of those who love him, who have been called according to his purposes to cultivate renewal and wholeness in this world.

This Kingdom-minded service offers to bring life and redemption into our stories. It's not just people who will be redeemed, which is no little thing, but our workplaces, schools, hospitals, and marketplaces as well. All things, industries, and economics realigned with the holy workings of Christ.

As I acknowledge my life as it is right now, I'm not surprised God gave Lindsey and I the little nudge to buy a house we could restore. Our home has certainly transformed from a ruddy worn-down thing built a hundred years ago into a living and growing abode. The restoration of Parkwood was a small reflection of what God wants to do in our lives. He wants to take our stories, that may be beaten up and weary, and breathe life and beauty into them again.

Little did we know our old row house would become so much more than just a shelter of wood and stone. Our home is not just some crash pad living quarters with an address. It is a living, breathing, and growing sanctuary where our life explodes with the goodness of God. Every single day, this little haven wraps its walls and windows around us and invites us to explore, adventure, love, work, and grieve.

It is the home base where we serve and love one another. Its doors swing wide for neighbors to come and stay for a while. A place to rest. This little home on Parkwood holds memories, longings, securities and insecurities, laughter, tears, and blood. It's filled with the scent of home-cooked meals, coffee, and pastries. Lindsey tends the gardens, flowers, and vegetation. We serve and pursue our marriage within these walls. Lord-willing, this is the little kingdom my kids will grow up and flourish in.

Parkwood has become a heavenly refuge for my family. It invokes emotions and feelings of delight and wonder. It is the lighthouse that draws us in from life's cold, hard, and rainy experiences when we need to rest and feel encouraged. It holds the smell of coffee in the morning as I sit in our corner chair watching the seasons ramble on.

It bears the pitter patter of tiny human footsteps learning to walk on century-old creaking hardwood floors. Parkwood creates a nostalgia of home like Christmas lights and garland hung on the portico. It welcomes us to gather and linger at the dinner table with those we love. It invites us to delight in good laughter and conversation, wine, and a warm meal.

Participating in the restoration of Parkwood has shown me that Jesus longs to bring revival and rebirth into our stories. He has the intention to take our lives, that have been broken and bent by the fall, and breathe life and beauty into them again. Where his act of renewal, no matter how big or small, ripples into other acts of restoration.

The Kingdom of God, full of goodness and grace, is a cosmic domino effect set in motion by Jesus and carried out through his people. We're invited to participate with him in the renaissance of the here and now. The revival of our own hearts and the lives around us, bringing hope to a weary and wandering world.

Chapter Fourteen
Grief and Glory

I 've never seen the walls fall down in my parents' life like I did that afternoon. They were flustered beyond anything I had ever known as a little kid. It was as if a flash-bang grenade detonated in the living room, and we were fumbling for something to hold onto. They were trying to make sense of everything and keep from breaking down.

Eugene, my grandfather, had just collapsed in the long gravel driveway of their house on Bandy Road. He suffered a stroke and lied there, face-down outside the house until help came. His blue-jean hat sprawled on the drive with his eyeglasses cracked and pressed against the ground. Life was still pulsing in his body, but dwindling as the ambulance hauled him away.

As a little kid, the people who raise you often seem like superheroes. They're bigger, taller, and stronger in nature. They always seem to have the answers and are the main authority in childhood and adolescence. In the mind of a child, the people who raise them take on the role of guardian, protector, and defender. They're the people that are supposed to be trustworthy, the source of provision, and a safe place. For the most part, adults are the mainstay in a person's younger years— at least, this is how it should be.

After all, they're older, more mature, and have more life experience. In a kid's mind, adults are supposed to be the ones who aren't scared of the monster in the closet or the bullies of life. That's how I thought of things, but this entire perspective changed the day my grandfather collapse. Or perhaps the doorway into heartache was open all along and I had never stepped into that room.

The hours surrounding my 73-year-old grandfather's death are clouded and blurry. I can only see faint images in my mind like Polaroids rather than a reel-to-reel video player. I do remember the spectrum of emotions in the room. A five-year-old kid grappling with his first personal experience of a loved one's passing. Something that only existed in the margins or movies had made its way onto the front pages of my story.

I remember looking into Eugene's eyes one last time. I can recall the dimly lit room, his hoarse breathing, and failing body on the hospital bed. I can faintly remember hearing my parents' voices shaking. The sound of weeping and the repeated goodbyes. The crushing weight of life was coming to an end for someone we loved. My young childlike spirit was being marred by death. I was experiencing the end of a beloved story, and I had no clue what to do with myself and the whirlwind inside my chest.

My grandfather's death revealed a frailty and vulnerability I never knew existed. I saw this particularly clear in my parents as a depth of emotions began to bubble to the surface. Heartache rippled through our family and left us lost for words.

In a little boy's eyes, the people who were the most solid and strong in the world were, in an instant, rattled with pain, anger, confusion, and sorrow. If my invincible parents could be grieved so deeply by death, what hope was there for me? How could my childlike emotions ever overcome or rationalize such sorrow and grief?

My small understanding of life fell short in answering the questions I asked. I had no language or knowledge around something like death. I was disoriented, and my vocabulary couldn't explain what was unfolding. But what I could comprehend was that disappointment, death, and pain had left its mark on humanity. Regardless of age, race, sexuality, finances, or any other identifier, all people are clearly susceptible to grief and sorrow, I realized. Death was a staple of humanity that I would inevitably experience throughout my story.

The sting of disappointment and pain have come in small and big ways through my life. Being laughed at on the playground, being left out of the popular crowd, the first break-up, getting cut from the baseball team, receiving the rejection letter, not getting the job, being misunderstood, being bullied, and the death of more loved ones. I have gone through circumstances, both menial and monumental, that wrenched apart my inner world.

Life constantly reminds us that it is tough and not partial to who you are, what you have, or what you do. Chances are high that you have your own running list of ways you've been let down and disappointed by life. We've all experienced loads of emotional, physical, and spiritual pain.

To be honest, I'm not even sure what to do with it at times. I wrestle with how to handle the continual onslaught of resistance and suffering. We live in damaging realities every day that can make us question ourselves, our faith, pressure us to live feebly, and even believe lies about who God is. Suffering and grief are heavy weights to bear. They're deeply hefty experiences and emotions that can be absolutely crushing. How in the world are we supposed to live our lives considering this? How do we navigate the experiences that wreck us? Where in the world is God in all of this and how does faith fit in?

These are the questions I've been wrestling with for so many years. I've been trying to wrap my head and heart around the realities of trials and tragedy. I've desperately wanted to have an anchor for my soul in the storms of life. Especially when I know that trouble and suffering aren't going to ever go away.

I stepped out of a meeting several years ago and took a call from Lindsey. My hands immediately started shaking as my nervous system began to send warning signs that something was wrong. She told me her body had been showing heavier symptoms of a miscarriage that morning, so we rushed to the hospital. Lindsey was immediately sent back to be seen by the OB-GYN. I felt nauseous as I said prayers to God like flares in the sky. I begged for a healthy wholesome diagnosis. We held onto hope as best as we could, but our hearts felt heavy with uncertainty and fear.

We spent the rest of the day weeping over the loss of our second child. I'll never forget how broken my life seemed at that moment. I even felt a physiological response to the inward disruption. My face was flushed red from a thousand emotions, my breathing was different, I couldn't stop sweating, and my legs felt unsteady. I was angry with God and felt as though everything Jesus had ever told me was a lie. I fought against the bitterness that assailed me. It felt like a wave of sorrow crashed upon the shores of our lives and left everything wrecked and ruined.

The time after our miscarriage was uneasy. Lindsey dealt with the lingering physical ramifications in her body along with the ache in her heart. I wrestled with all sorts of emotional and spiritual baggage. It came in waves. Some days were better than others. It didn't take much to bring our eyes to tears. A conversation, glance, or even a song had the power to bring us right back to the source of our pain.

We were grieving the loss of life. The sting of death continually prodding us throughout the months to come. Our hearts ached knowing we would never get to see our little embryo grow and flourish into full human life. Our hearts lamented the loss, both the present and the future, because our stories would never know the life that could have been. We wouldn't know the joy of holding that baby in our arms, feel its skin, hear its cry, or wonder at the baby's smallness and goodness. Everything we envisioned for this child's life had ended too soon.

I really had to reckon with a lot of life's pain, disappointment, and loss when that happened. I had to really confront who I was, what I believed, and how I would let things shape me. It caused me to question my faith and relationship with Jesus. I had to decide what I would stake my life on. I wrestled with God like Jacob on the side of the Jordan. I argued and pleaded with him like the Psalmist. I renounced him at times like Peter. My heart ran wild and weary.

I stumbled homeward like the younger prodigal son in the Gospel of Luke and was greeted the same. A loving father already on the horizon running to me with warmth and gentleness. His heart provoked with a sadness that far outweighed my own grieving.

Jesus' response to me was a reminder of a moment in the Chronicles of Narnia series, when the young boy character, Digory, faces Aslan (the Christ-like figure) over Digory's dying mother. Digory says to the great lion,

> "'But please, please—won't you—can't you give me something that will cure Mother?' Up till then he had been looking at the Lion's great feet and the huge claws on them; now, in his despair, he looked up at its face. What he saw surprised him as much as anything in his whole life. For the tawny face was bent down near his own and (wonder of wonders) great shining tears stood in the Lion's eyes. They were such big, bright tears compared with Digory's own that for a moment

he felt as if the Lion must really be sorrier about
his Mother than he was himself.".[1]

I found no scolding and indifference from Jesus. But instead, he met my heart with the patience and tenderness it desperately needed. I didn't find answers to all my questions, but I did swim deeper into the story of God's grace. This was a significant shift in my life and faith.

I was knocked out cold by sorrow's right hook and then caught in the arms of God's compassion. Life threw me into the coexistence of loss and love. Misery and mercy. Pain and peace. This is when I began to recognize that without a doubt life is marked by grief and glory.

As Christians, we endure through life by rooting ourselves in the grace and glory of Jesus. We place our hope in the one who will not abandon us. Scripture holds the tension of hardship and joy. Our spirits must remain tethered to the truth of God's faithfulness during turbulent times.

Paul encourages us to rejoice and give thanks in all circumstances (1 Thessalonians 5:16-18). The Psalmist emboldens us to rejoice and be glad (Psalm 118:24). Nehemiah reinforces that the joy of the Lord is our strength (Nehemiah 8:10). Jesus himself reminds us that in this world we will have trouble, trials, and tribulation, but to take heart for he has overcome the world (John 16:33).

We take heart because joy isn't rooted in something that will perish or fade. The heart of Christ does not ebb and flow like the ocean tide. He does not falter like everything else in this world.

Biblical joy is not worldly happiness. Worldly happiness can be taken from you in an instant. You can be riding the high of happiness only to have it pulled out from underneath you moments later. And while happiness is a good and wonderful thing, it is also fragile and can break very easily.

The Christian distinction and definition of joy is much different. Joy can be punched in the face, pummeled to the ground, spit on, and beaten, yet joy remains strong and resolute. The worst of the worst can be thrown up against us and our joy can remain.

Paul paints this picture for us in his second letter to the Corinthians when he expresses: "That is why, for Christ's sake, I delight in weaknesses, in insults, in hardships, in persecutions, in difficulties. For when I am weak, then I am strong" (2 Corinthians 12:10 NIV). This reflects true Christian joy— something much deeper than happiness that transcends circumstances. Joy anchors us in truth so we can move beyond the gloomy night into the dawn of God's goodness.

Our experience of joy is directly tied to where we place our hope and love. If our hope is placed in something that can't bear its weight, we'll have no real shot at experiencing true joy. And I'm sure we've all placed our hope in the wrong things at times, ultimately letting ourselves down.

If our hope is tied to our spouse, we might end up devastated when they break our trust. If it's placed in our jobs, we may become bitter when it falls apart. If we place our hope in friendships, we're opening ourselves up to be stung by betrayal. If our purpose in life is in our kids, we'll be deeply let down when they disobey us. If our bank account is our only hope, we may be rocked if it's drained by a recession. Whatever we tie our joy to, will determine the strength of our hearts.

When the purpose of who we are is planted in the wrong object, we're bound to be disappointed. The Bible emphasizes how faith and hope must be placed in Jesus. Anything else is unsteady and unable to sustain us. The only person in the cosmos who can bear the weight of our lives is Jesus.

We can observe this in the way Jesus responds to grief, anguish, death, and pain. We see his very heart for humanity in his gentleness with us. Not only that, but in Christ's death on the cross, the manner in which he went, and his glorious resurrection show he can handle everything we bring to him.

Despite our messiness, Jesus only draws nearer; it is his nature. Dane Ortlund writes this about the heart of Jesus for sinners and sufferers, "The deeper into weakness and suffering and testing we go, the deeper Christ's solidarity with us. As we go down into pain and anguish, we are descending ever deeper into Christ's very heart, not away from it."[2] The process of moving through grief and pain takes us into the very personhood of Jesus. Where we will find his true spirit for us, which is full of loving kindness.

It is through enduring life's hardships that we draw closer to God. The one we can lay our lives on. Jesus can carry the weight of your burdens, shame, and pain just as he carried the weight of the cross. The God of the universe has the power and might to have the very forces of hell crash upon him and live. Jesus is the haven where we can place our hope and it will hold. There is no other option.

So, as we endure the various tensions of our existence, take whatever steps you can to live into the joy of Jesus, which can vary in matter and method. Joy isn't this perpetual smile or enthusiasm that hides what is going on underneath the surface. It is not some sort of facade to cover up the reality of what we're experiencing.

Joy can sometimes look like a sob-soaked pillowcase. Sometimes joy is praying the same prayer repeatedly. Sometimes it is just choosing to get out of bed in the morning when it feels like climbing a mountain. Although joy can take many different shapes, this sentiment remains the same: the joy of Jesus is deeper and richer than worldly happiness and transcends beyond life's worst experiences.

In her book Prayer in the Night, Tish Warren shares this wonderful thought, "Of course the ever-present reality of grief does not mean that we feel sad all the time. Grief is as much a part of us as our circulatory system or our middle name, but we are complex people and we can, and do, hold both joy and grief together because they both witness to things that are true. Thankfully even in a wounded world, we still taste glory, adventure, exuberance, and even euphoria."[3] This is the paradox we engage every day of our lives and sometimes the scale feels like it's tipping more towards grief, while at other moments it's easier to live in joy. As we hold both realities together, we come to understand that sadness and joy do coexist.

This is another marker of a life of fullness. When we consider the life of Jesus, the most human of humans, he too experienced the tension of grief and joy. Jesus himself felt the lowest of lows and the highest of highs. He knows the full spectrum of emotions involved in a story that includes sorrow, grief, exuberance, and joy. An overflowing life is a story that experiences the entire scope of human emotions and interactions.

So, in everything you're going through, however painful and disappointing, remember this; we have Christ as an anchor for our souls. The only one who can hold our hurt. To the little boy who just lost his grandfather, there is hope. For the mother and father who have lost their child, your sorrow will coexist with joy in this life or the next.

To the one who has been betrayed, there is one who will never betray you. For the person who has been abused and discarded, there is one who calls you lovely and adored. To the person who weeps, there is one who weeps with you. His name is Jesus, and everything in him pulses with love, comfort, and compassion for our aching hearts.

Chapter Fifteen

Cascades and Canyons

Lindsey and I went out west several years ago to unplug and get off the grid for several days. It was in the first couple years of our marriage while we were in our mid-twenties and hadn't had kids yet. We had just moved into a little apartment on Floyd Avenue in Richmond after being in Charlotte, North Carolina for several years. I said a tearful and grateful goodbye to Young Life. Lindsey had left her job as a teacher at a local high school. We were in the middle of discovering a new chapter in our stories, exploring new opportunities, and uncovering more of what direction God was leading us.

I remember being wildly curious about what life should look like with all the change we were facing. A significant amount of my story had been wrapped around work and vocation. To a degree, I think I even had an unhealthy relationship with work.

So much of my contentment and identity had been tied to my success in different jobs. I felt uneasy and nervous about what work was supposed to look like.

A part of me felt pressure to have it all figured out, but I couldn't have been further away from an answer. Enough time had passed since graduating college; my thirties weren't all that far off. Wasn't I supposed to be climbing the promotional ladder and settling into a career at this point? At the very least, I felt this cultural strain to feel settled down, but I honestly felt an apprehension with everything.

The truth is, God was just beginning to help me understand what his true design for vocation looks like. More importantly, Jesus started to reveal how transformative work can be in a person's life. I kept wrestling with curiosity—asking God how my job should play out in my story.

I wanted to lean more into this, dodge distractions, and tune into what Jesus was initiating in my heart. So, Lindsey and I booked our tickets, packed our bags, and caught a flight for Colorado at the end of that summer. I needed some space to dodge the interruptions and let my soul have some room to wander.

We shut down our devices and let the vivid terrain and backdrop speak to us. Lindsey and I ventured through the alluring western landscape of arid deserts, river canyons, and snow-covered mountains. The higher altitude made for beautiful, sun-filled days and cooler, comfortable evenings. We felt the freedom to indulge the wilderness and allow our hearts to connect with creation with our lungs full of mile-high air.

One of our treks into Rocky Mountain National Park was particularly memorable to me. We caught a trailhead and hiked headfirst into the four hundred fifteen square miles of protected mountains, forests, and alpine tundra. The scenery and landscape were captivating, but despite the beauty around me, I remember being stuck in my head. I remember feeling riddled with thoughts about work and career paths back home. The tension I wanted to leave in Richmond had followed me to Colorado.

We kept hiking through the Glacier Gorge trailhead toward Sky Pond, which takes you past at least three waterfalls and a beautiful set of cascades. I was allured by the Colorado terrain one moment and then pulled back into my anxiety with work the next. I felt the need to shake my racing mind. I began to pray and give everything over to Jesus. I offered up to him my worry and apprehension while loosening my white-knuckled-grip on my future.

The vast landscape of Colorado became a wide-open frontier where I couldn't hide from God anymore. I simply continued to plead with Jesus to bring me peace and clarity about my future and what lies ahead with my work. I put 1,734 miles of distance between me and what had been plaguing me back home. Sure enough, through the rush of rivers, cascades, and canyons, Jesus began to show me more of his heart for vocation and his vision for my future.

His voice came gently to my heart with reassurance and enlightenment. My focus began to shift outwards at the nature around me, its intrinsic beauty, and the hands that created it all.

I began to understand that God was the first toiler and workman. His words and actions in creation are the first expressions of craftsmanship and labor in scripture.

With God's landscape of creation encircling me, I began to reflect on Genesis–considering more deeply the relationship between humanity and work. God brought my attention to the creation mandate, which is his command to subdue, cultivate, and have dominion over the earth. In the very wake of creation, God instills in humanity the profound significance of occupation. It is our God-given agency to work, keep, and cultivate the world around us.

My experience engaging God during this time away wasn't some religious stunt. It wasn't artificial or fabricated. It was a longing to dodge the noise and retreat away with Jesus. If anything, it reflected Jesus himself when he would steal away to the olive groves of the Middle Eastern countryside to be alone with his father.

I needed to shake the fog of my questions and get alone with God. Do I believe I could've stepped out into my backyard or a park nearby to commune with the Maker of mountains? Yes, of course, but for this instance, my heart led to Colorado and in that frontier, Jesus unraveled my concerns and questions. It was almost as if I needed to see the grandiosity of his handiwork in order to gain insight into biblical principles for vocation.

We hiked our way around more of Colorado and then set our sights on leaving. For many weeks after returning home, I would recount in my life the ways the Lord had met me. The vast landscape of the wild, wild west revealed to me more of the person of Jesus and brought me peace and clarity about my everyday work. It was as if creation had the power to reflect to me the character and career of God.

It's been many years since that trip, yet Jesus is still teaching me so much about one's work in life. He's continuing to reveal the significance that business, occupation, work, and labor have in the Christian life. I'm learning more and more of the intrinsic value behind how we spend the hours of our day in our jobs and commissions.

All work looks different, but despite the variations people will likely spend more than 90,000 hours of their life working. This equals 21 percent of our total waking hours over a seventy-six-year lifespan, assuming an average of eight hours of sleep a night. According to those metrics almost a quarter of our lives will be spent in a workplace, which I think emphasizes the significance placed on our vocations.

No task is too small either. In fact, regardless of the proportion of the task, each activity we engage holds boundless value and dignity in God's eyes. Timothy Keller, in his writings in Every Good Endeavor, says, "The material creation was made by God to be developed, cultivated, and cared for in an endless number of ways through human labor. But even the simplest of these ways is important. Without them all, human life cannot flourish."[1] Note the word *all* in the last sentence. Every form of work, when pursued rightly, holds dignity and grace. So let this be an encouragement, regardless of what your activities are each day, that there is significant value in developing, cultivating, and caring for the common good in what you do.

When we realize that our work is an avenue by which we bring about human flourishing, we will begin to consider all work more heavenly. This will also help us wrap our minds around the dependency we share with one another's professions. Tish Warren says, "Our lives depend on one another's toil. We need each other. We need others to do their work well."[2] Did you get that? We all have a reliance on communal work. In order to really thrive we must depend on each other's toil.

In a world of instant gratification, big box stores, and online shopping, it's incredibly easy to lose sense of our communal dependence. Yet, when we slow down and realize how all work helps our lives function, it brings into perspective our need for one other. And not just each other's work, but for each of us to do our work excellently. The way to serve God best in our vocations is to do our work as best as it can be done.

When I consider this and look at my work-life over the years I noticeably realize that those biblical principles of vocation hold true. Even just reflecting on my work as a real estate professional highlights the significance of bringing my work before God. From the initial spark of the relationship, my clients are relying upon my expertise and services for their real estate needs.

I can love, care, and serve people as they're making one of the biggest decisions of their lives. For me to take things lightly and not approach it with integrity would be out of line with scripture. Am I an imperfect person that has faults and failures? Of course, but the sentiment is true, there is substantial dignity in our jobs and doing them with excellence. There is immense dignity in social work, respite care, stay-at-home parents, bankers, construction workers, dentists, cashiers, stocking associates, bookkeepers, servers, and medical assistants. The list goes on, but regardless it is all meaningful and needed.

As a real estate professional, I've learned to cultivate my business around scripture. I work toward excellence and glorifying Jesus through serving the community. I've learned to lean on plenty of other professionals to get the job done well. I've depended on lenders, contractors, other agents, house cleaners, moving companies, title companies, carpenters, painters, and more. I've experienced first-hand my need for the community in order to provide the best level of service possible. My heart behind the work matters to God.

This gives us freedom, whatever our roles, to live with purpose and providence. It provides our daily tasks with deeper and richer meaning. Martin Luther is noted for saying, "Every occupation has its own honor before God. Ordinary work is a divine vocation or calling. In our daily work no matter how important or mundane we serve God by serving the neighbor and we also participate in God's on-going providence for the human race."[3] The pressure is off. We get to rest in the assurance that we work for the divine. Our vocational calling in Jesus is bringing forth the Kingdom of God on earth as it is in heaven.

So regardless of how mundane and menial our jobs may seem each day, they are (in essence) building brick by brick the foundation for human flourishing. Our work can bring love, joy, peace, patience, kindness, generosity, faithfulness, gentleness, and self-control into our workplaces. Our work reflects Genesis as we cultivate the glory of God. John Mark Comer, in his book

Garden City, says, "Our job is to make the invisible God visible—to mirror and mimic what he is like to the world. We can glorify God by doing our work in such a way that we make the invisible God visible by what we do and how we do it."[4]

So many industries are just about making more money, having more things, and attaining more awards or titles. Because of this, it's even more important to not lose sight of what really matters in our work. It grounds our motivation and impulses. It keeps us tethered to Jesus and helps us honor him through our toil.

Sure, making money, having stuff, and achieving things is fine and good. But the ultimate marker of our work should be glorifying God and cultivating his Kingdom here on earth. This should be our indicator of faithfulness, not the promotion we get from our bosses.

As I write this, Lindsey and I have been in the trenches of parenthood. We are living through many sleepless nights and foggy days with a one-year-old where the mind just isn't firing on all cylinders. It's a combination of being so deeply in love with our daughter while also being drained of ourselves. With that said, we are expecting another child this year. I'm nervous how much our lives are going to change again, but at the same time I'm wonderfully excited for our growing family.

In the first several years of becoming a parent, you truly begin to realize the impact you have on your child's growth and understanding of the world. Parents have monumental and lasting influence on their children. Our children look like us, sound like us, and even act like us at times. It's terrifying really, yet such a wonderful reflection of Christian spirituality. And as I witness Lindsey in motherhood, I'm struck yet again with the Bible's mandate on labor and service.

It's awe-inspiring to see Lindsey's life deepen and widen for our little girl. Lindsey steps into the God-given call on her life every single day. She is on the clock 24/7 with Evelyn, working heartily to raise her in goodness and grace. Lindsey longs to see our child raised up in love and kindness. This is an extension and expression of her current role and calling, which again reminds me of the dignity of all kinds of work.

As we go about our toils on earth, Jesus is the one we must look to for assurance and approval. He is the one who establishes our work and defines its significance. We see that God was a gardener in Genesis, cultivating the earth. We see that God in the New Testament was a carpenter. Jesus gave himself in a trade for his community. The woodworker from Nazareth lived out his vocation in the Middle East until his time would come to take up his greatest labor, which would bring us salvation. I imagine Christ as a cultivator and laborer of the Kingdom, serving and stewarding the community around him.

Let us remember we are made in God's image and bear his creativity and purpose for work and toil. God offers us important and incredible assignments to pursue within our stories. Regardless of our placement in the working world, God has deep purpose and providence for us. Jesus wants to make the glory and goodness of his Kingdom known through the work of the mechanic, technician, custodian, business owner, artist, and everyone in between.

Chapter Sixteen

Echoes of Eden

I stood with my mouth wide open in wonder beneath the 1,113 stained-glass windowpanes of Sainte-Chapelle. I was in a gothic-styled chapel located in the medieval Palais de la Cité in Paris, France. This royal chapel features fifteen stained-glass windowpanes, each stretching fifty feet high, depicting scenes from the Old and New Testament.

These massive window illustrations recounted the history of the world. Hues of blue as colorful as the ocean. Tints of sunlit reds, oranges, and golds danced across the panes like flames. Shades of emerald-like evergreen pine dazzled from the shards of glass. The stained windowpanes glowed from the sunshine above, which made everything look like a swirling sea of jewels. I stood there feeling insignificant and meek amongst such beauty and artistry.

Sainte-Chapelle remains one of my favorite places to revel upon the beauty of creativity in Paris, which is saying a lot with such grand cathedrals and monuments around every corner of the City of Light. The Louvre, Eiffel Tower, Cathedral of Notre Dame, Arc De Triomphe, Musee d'Orsay, Palace de Versailles, and the Sacre-Coeur are a few that come to mind. However, there are thousands of other sights and scenes to witness in the small byways of Paris. A city filled with brilliance and mastery.

Lindsey and I took two trips to Europe before Evelyn was born. In our first trip we had traveled to France, Greece, and Italy. After returning to the states, we had this lingering desire to travel back across the pond as soon as life would allow. Life the following year gave us the chance to slip away for another few weeks of travel. So, we jumped at the opportunity, booked our flights, and started packing.

It was early autumn when we landed in London that year. The buzz of adventure was already palpable as we stepped off the plane in Heathrow. We rode the tube to our station in Farringdon and strolled to our stay on the corner of St. John's Square and Clerkenwell. We quickly tossed our bags in the room and headed back out into the rush and thrill that only a foreign city can give you.

I can close my eyes and remember the sounds of double-decker buses and little black cabs rushing down Fulham Road through Chelsea toward Westminster Abbey. I can hear laughter and paddle boats rippling across the water of the Serpentine in Hyde Park. I can smell the aroma of freshly brewed coffee and buttered pastries floating through the doors of the Old Dutch

Cafe. I can taste the crisp golden notes of a cold lager in the Red Lion surrounded by cheerful London locals, and I can recall the morning scent of freshly cut tulips, marigold, and jasmine from the Columbia Road flower market.

The novelty and customs of London were amazing to us. Centuries of history, architecture, and values enveloped us. It was so enthralling to gallivant through cities we'd only dreamed of visiting while relying on all forms of transportation imaginable: planes, trains, ferries, subways, bikes, taxis, and our own two feet. I deeply resonate with the words of George Bailey in It's a Wonderful Life, "The three most exciting sounds in the world are anchor chains, plane motors, and train whistles."[1]

Over the course of those weeks abroad, we spent time in Holland, Belgium, England, and France. We stayed in a houseboat on a canal in Bruges, where we rested to the rock and sway of the Belgic water. In Amsterdam, we marveled at the artistic heritage, elaborate canal systems, and row houses with gabled facades. We engaged in the biking culture, which was so ripe with neighborliness.

The vast assortment of cuisine and libations in each city brought such savory indulgence. All the places we explored and discovered had such charm and elegance. Time after time, we would be hit with such exuberance of what we were experiencing that we'd just smile at each other, laugh, and kiss.

But the train ride slows down, the airplane lands, and the taxi stops. At some point, the trip comes to an end, and for most of us, we return to our everyday lives in an everyday world. We get back to our jobs, responsibilities, and daily activities. As much as we wish the adventure would last a little longer, it always eventually wanes.

I used to think adventure, revelry, and wonder only existed outside of my small, daily domain. I believed great experiences could only be found on the extraordinary frontier of travel, uncertainty, and enterprise. I had tasted the delicacy of Italian fare and wine in Greece. I had walked the ancient streets of Athens and seen the blue domes of the Mediterranean. I had marveled at the immensity of St. Paul's and St. Peter's. I sat beneath the fresco ceiling of the Sistine Chapel. I stood amazed by the cliffside villages of the Amalfi Coast along with its pebbled beaches, lemon groves, and cafes.

But this was only for a short stint. I would return home to find my ordinary life moving back to center stage. Daily responsibilities, rhythms, and normalcy welcomed me home like an old friend. For the most part, there would be no historic wonders to behold or sights to see. Just the everyday common happenings of my story to experience.

I was back to the same familiar city, friends, church, and family. I must admit it troubled me at times that my daily life didn't have these grand sights or novel experiences. My life seemed black and white compared to the technicolor I experienced for what I thought was adventure. I questioned my everyday circumstances. I wrestled with life and its commonness. I felt as though I was missing out on something. I scuffled with God.

I remember having a rough spell spiritually and emotionally during the summer before Evelyn was born. I was stuck in this colorless cycle of monotony, wondering if the normalcy of life would eventually just overtake and crush me. My faith, which had always been the grounding anchor in my life, felt like it had been etched away.

Doubt and anxiety seemed to creep over me quite often. I struggled to believe the fundamental truths of Christianity. The Lord seemed to be uninterested in the current state of my heart. He felt quiet, distant, and apathetic. The exact opposite of who I had known him to be.

This was a confusing time in my life. Most of what I knew or heard growing up in Christian circles suddenly seemed distorted. Nothing added up from what I was reading in scripture with what I was experiencing in my soul. How could God's heart be for me, while he simultaneously allowed me to wrestle with this turbulence in my inner being?

I eventually conceded that some of my questions would go on unanswered. Tish Warren writes, "God did not keep bad things from happening to God himself and that God who does not keep bad things from happening, is also clear that he makes good things happen."[2] This seemed profoundly true and so I began to base my questions on it.

If God allows bad and good things to happen, then he may just allow my soul to feel barren for reasons I might not understand at the time. I remember holding onto close friends and family to buoy my heart. Those closest, sitting and weeping with me, reminded me that all things do pass in one way or another. My dark night of the soul was illuminated by those who loved me and continued to show me the heart of Jesus when I could not see it myself.

My daughter Evelyn was born in late October of that same year. We brought her home to Parkwood surrounded by autumn leaves and a tangerine sky. I'll never forget those very first days with her. Crisp autumn air drafting through the open windowpane, Peter Sandberg's Scandinavian Jazz record playing from my phone, and my journal and a few books strewn on the bedside table. Life was unhurried and naps were plentiful. We took things slow and delighted in our newborn baby girl.

Evelyn was and remains a hurricane of love, splendor, and heaven in my life. Everything within reach of her seems to feel the gravity of her existence. She has a propensity for curiosity, which always leads her into discovery and exploration. Evelyn is no stranger to her wonderful heart and remarkable emotions, which she feels and expresses very deeply. She is tender in spirit and has always served as heaven's herald for my wandering heart. God remarkably used her at that time in my life to bring me back to him.

This is when I realized that there is something more breathtaking and beautiful than the likes of the Eiffel Tower, Positano's coastline, Venice's canals, Florence's Duomo, or Rome's Colosseum. She currently stands twenty-five inches tall, has dark brown eyes, and a laugh that can soften any hardened heart into molten lava. And I get to wake up and wonder at Evelyn's brilliance every ordinary day—where God uses her life to awaken my spirit to the here and now of a life of fullness.

I get the opportunity to take delight and pleasure in the most common experiences of my everyday life. Jesus has continued to strip away misconceptions and replaced them with a renewed understanding that life, wherever I am, has deep beauty and purpose. I didn't have to travel to find meaningful experiences. I could have them right here and now.

It may sound crazy, and maybe you already understand this in your faith, but I had the wrong impression of how God allowed me to encounter and worship him. For some reason, I thought that if the moment wasn't grand, it wasn't glorious. Now I see that every day, God invites me into a relationship with him where I get the opportunity to respond to his love. Through this, all things become glorious.

A slow stroll around my block in Richmond through our local park with a peaceful lake helps me breathe and witness the creativity of God with each passing season. The scent of freshly brewed coffee rising from the French press can awaken my senses to Jesus. The scratch of a vinyl record filling the room with cadence and rhythm. The touch of a loved one, a kiss, and a hug reminds us that we're not alone. The sound of crickets and flashes of lightning bugs on a warm summer's eve have the power to point us towards the creator.

A warm crackling fire in the hearth can bring from our lungs a hallelujah. Freshly fallen snow and the silence it casts can slow our souls to rest. The deep, velvety red of a glass of wine can bring about thankfulness and merriment. Falling into cool sheets at the end of the day can bring a sigh of reprieve.

As we tune into our lives and what God is doing, we will uncover the plot of our life's story and the heavenly opportunities to connect with Jesus in each moment. All of this and so much more are the markings of an abundant life. Each passing moment of life is an interaction and encounter with the Maker himself. A chance to cherish what's before our very eyes.

There is great significance in becoming more aware of the wonder and beauty of God around us. Leaning into the purposes of Jesus within our daily lives matters so much more than we know. The simple way to do this is by looking and listening for his encouragement and invitations.

One reason we miss out on God's work in our lives is because we're not even looking for it to begin with. Our hearts aren't in the right place, we're distracted, or we're busy. We miss the work of the Holy Spirit, and we miss the Lord speaking into our lives.

During a conversation Jesus had with his disciples, he sheds light on the people who aren't in a place to see, hear, and understand the matters of the Kingdom of heaven. Jesus quotes the prophet Isaiah, "For this people's heart has become calloused; they hardly hear with their ears, and they have closed their eyes. Otherwise, they might see with their eyes, hear with their ears, understand with their hearts and turn, and I would heal them" (Matthew 13:15 NIV). Jesus is expressing the importance of having our hearts in the right place in order to receive the healing we so desperately need. The healing and transformation that comes through knowing God.

There is a way of delighting in God and loving him in return. Our lives can experience and encounter Jesus like our closest friend. Growing open to the Spirit in our lives will fan into flame the offer of relationship with God in Jesus. It is a way by which we grow in our need and awareness of the Lord throughout the day.

It is through our unity with Jesus that we experience a life of fullness, despite how circumstances may unravel daily. Life with Jesus is as accessible and personal as Psalm 23 (NIV),

> "The Lord is my shepherd, I lack nothing. He makes me lie down in green pastures, he leads me beside quiet waters, he refreshes my soul. He guides me along the right paths for his name's sake. Even though I walk through the darkest valley, I will fear no evil, for you are with me; your rod and your staff, they comfort me. You prepare a table before me in the presence of my enemies. You anoint my head with oil; my cup overflows. Surely your goodness and love will follow me all the days of my life, and I will dwell in the house of the Lord forever."

Jesus also said, "Look! I stand at the door and knock. If you hear my voice and open the door, I will come in, and we will share a meal together as friends" (Revelation 3:20 NLT). All of this and more is freely offered to us through relationship and union with Jesus.

Unfortunately, we often move through our stories exhausted and distracted. It makes sense that we miss the divine in the daily. We don't practice slowing down, breathing, and finding silence to experience Jesus at the heart of it all.

Our lifestyles rush right past the purposes of God without so much as a glance of care or understanding. To breathe, recognize, and realign with Jesus is to press the pause button more often in our stories. It doesn't need to be some long carved out time, but rather just turning our gaze back to glory.

I encourage you to take inventory of your life and think more deeply about what you discover. Grow in your awareness of connecting with the Lord throughout your day. Take a glance at the check engine light of your heart. If it's flashing, pay attention.

Bring your cares to Jesus because he wants to be deeply involved in your life and the matters at hand. We may not be able to see it because of the predictability by which we live, but Jesus is at work in our wonderfully ordinary stories. The closer we look at our lives, the more magnified God's plot for our stories will become.

The degree to which our lives are turned toward Jesus is the degree to which we'll begin to see, hear, and understand the heavenly around us. The more in-tune we are with God, the more we'll notice the beauty in our stories. Our wonder and thirst for life will be shaped and filled by the ever-flowing rivers and waterfalls of God's grace.

Our days will still consist of chores, emails, dishes, pets, and taking out the trash. Yes, the predictability and commonness will remain, but the ordinary will begin to point us towards an extraordinary God. Awareness will allow our hearts to blossom and become more cognizant of the Lord's purpose and providence in our narratives.

Those boring emails can become avenues to care and correspond with a depleted coworker. Taking care of the house and raising kids becomes the channel of experiencing God's glory. The product or service you provide is no longer a means to an end, but a pathway to serve someone's well-being.

That dark night of my soul dissolved as the warmth and holiness of God's heart rose on it like the summer sun. I began to see my life's story in a new light. Similar to the quotable words of C.S. Lewis when he said, "I believe in Christianity as I believe that the sun has risen: not only because I see it, but because by it I see everything else."[3]

My renewed outlook on the nearness of Jesus and the access I was given to his heart became the new compass for my life. A story of faith, relationships, and wholeness is not illusive, far off, or over the next fence. Adventure, delight, and wonder are waiting to be uncovered in the ordinary moments of our lives. Jesus longs to give us great and glorious experiences with him where we can engage the King of creation in profound ways on small stages. No matter how you spin it, God offers us a million invitations in our everyday lives to be enchanted and loved by Jesus.

My life has come a long way over the past thirty some years. If you've stuck with me this far you now know how a beat-up, burned-out, lost, and lonely misfit like me was redeemed by the love of Jesus. How my life has been marked by relationships, community, children, dreams, embarrassment, guilt, grief, glory, and so much more. I'm learning to receive everything in my story, both wonderful, terrifying, and anything in between, as an opportunity to transform and flourish.

My story has been wonderfully ordinary, but I've come to realize that the mystery and magic of life is found in a deeply authentic relationship with Jesus. Where life is rooted in the adventure of faith played out in our everyday world. God is inviting us into this story of fullness with him here and now.

It is the echo of Eden.

And we get to say yes!

Acknowledgments

No readable book is ever written and published by one person alone. Feedback from my adored wife Lindsey; my lifelong comrade Landon Epperly; and my editor Abbey McLaughlin shaped this into a book worth picking up. Jordan Cotton, your creativity and artistry binds and covers this book more beautifully than I ever dared dream. Dad, Mom, and Lauren—my heart and story will forever be shaped by your love. Here's to the Original Gangsters—your companionship has been the wind at my back for over half of my life now. To all the wonderful people within these pages, thank you for the deep and profound impressions you've had upon my life. The stories are true.

Notes

Introduction:

1. Gregory Alan Isakov. (2016, August 31). *"The Stable Song" - Gregory Alan Isakov with the Colorado Symphony (official video)* [Video]. YouTube. https://www.youtube.com/watch?v=AqyAmmEkVvI

Chapter 1:

1. Eldredge, J. (2013). *Beautiful Outlaw: Experiencing the Playful, Disruptive, Extravagant Personality of Jesus* (Reprint). FaithWords.
2. Miller, D. (2003). *Blue Like Jazz: Nonreligious Thoughts on Christian Spirituality*. Thomas Nelson.
3. Warren, T. H., & Crouch, A. (2019). *Liturgy of the Ordinary: Sacred Practices in Everyday Life*. IVP Books.
4. *The Last Battle (Chronicles of Narnia) by C. S. Lewis (2008-01-02)*. (1888). HarperCollins.

Chapter 2:

1. Roosevelt, T. R. (n.d.). *Citizenship in a Republic*. Citizenship in a Republic, Paris, France.
2. Roosevelt, T. R. (n.d.-b). *Comparison Is The Thief Of Joy*. Unknown. https://www.goodreads.com/quotes/6471614-comparison-is-the-thief-of-joy

Chapter 3:

None

Chapter 4:

1. Miller, D. (2005). *Through Painted Deserts: Light, God, and Beauty on the Open Road*. Oliver-Nelson Books.
2. Tolkien, C., & Carpenter, H. (2000). *The Letters of J.R.R. Tolkien: A Selection*. Houghton Mifflin Company.
3. Keller, T., & Keller, K. (2011). *The Meaning of Marriage: Facing the Complexities of Commitment with the Wisdom of God*. Dutton.
4. Spurgeon, C. H. S. (n.d.). *The Unrivaled Friend*. Metropolitan Tabernacle Pulpit Volume 15. https://www.spurgeon.org/resource-library/sermons/the-unrivaled-friend/#flipbook/

Chapter 5:

1. Deutch, H. (Director). (2000, August 11). *The Replacements*. Warner Bros. Pictures.
2. Lewis, C. S. (2017). *The Four Loves* (Reissue). HarperOne.

Chapter 6:

1. Bob Clark (Director). (1983, November 18). *A Christmas Story*. Metro-Goldwyn-Mayer.
2. Augustine, S., & Pine-Coffin, R. S. (1961). *Confessions (Penguin Classics)* (Later Printing). Penguin Classics.
3. Keller, T. (2017, October 31). *How to Talk About Sin in a Postmodern Age*. The Gospel Coalition. https://www.thegospelcoalition.org/article/how-to-talk-sin-in-postmodern-age/
4. Erwin Raphael McManus (2006). "Uprising: A Revolution of the Soul", p.11, Thomas Nelson Inc
5. A quote from The Meaning of Marriage. (n.d.). https://www.goodreads.com/quotes/706587
6. Lewis, C. S., & Norris, K. (2015). *Mere Christianity* (Revised&Enlarged). HarperOne.
7. Eldredge, J. (2016). *Waking the Dead: The Secret to a Heart Fully Alive* (Expanded). Thomas Nelson.

Chapter 7:

1. Tolkien, J. R. R. (1994). *The Lord of the Rings Part Three The Return of the King*. Ballantine / Del Rey.
2. Coldplay. (2011, May 30). Coldplay - Fix You (Official Video) [Video]. YouTube. https://www.youtube.com/watch?v=k4V3Mo61fJM
3. Shakespeare, W. (2018). *Henry V*. CreateSpace Independent Publishing Platform.

Chapter 8:

1. Irenaeus, S. (2015). *Five Books Of S. Irenaeus: Bishop Of Lyons, Against Heresies*. Andesite Press.
2. McKelvey, D. K., & Bustard, N. (2020). *Every Moment Holy, Volume 1 (Pocket Edition)* (Illustrated). Rabbit Room.

Chapter 9:

1. Nouwen, H. J. M. (2006). *Bread for the Journey: A Daybook of Wisdom and Faith* (Reprint). HarperOne.
2. Sudeikis, J. (2020, August 14). *Ted Lasso*. Apple TV+. https://tv.apple.com/us/show/ted-lasso/umc.cmc.vtoh0mn0xn7t3c643xqonfzy
3. Willard, D. (2019). *Life Without Lack: Living in the Fullness of Psalm 23*. Thomas Nelson.
4. McKelvey, D. K., & Bustard, N. (2020). *Every Moment Holy, Volume 1 (Pocket Edition)* (Illustrated). Rabbit Room.

Chapter 10:

1. Tolkien, J. R. R. (1994). *The Lord of the Rings Part Three The Return of the King*. Ballantine / Del Rey.
2. McManus, E. R. (2015). *The Artisan Soul: Crafting Your Life into a Work of Art* (Reprint). HarperOne.

Chapter 11:

    1.   Goff, B. (2012). *Love Does: Discover a Secretly Incredible Life in an Ordinary World*. Thomas Nelson.

Chapter 12:

    1.   Ortlund, D. C. (2020). *Gentle and Lowly: The Heart of Christ for Sinners and Sufferers*. Crossway Books.

    2.   Ortlund, D. C. (2020). *Gentle and Lowly: The Heart of Christ for Sinners and Sufferers*. Crossway Books.

    3.   Tolkien, J. (2012a). *The Fellowship Of The Ring: Being the First Part of The Lord of the Rings (The Lord of the Rings, 1)* (Reissue). William Morrow Paperbacks.

    4.   Daniels, G. (Director). (2005, March 24). *The Office (American TV series)*.

    5.   Comer, J. M., & Ortberg, J. (2019). *The Ruthless Elimination of Hurry: How to Stay Emotionally Healthy and Spiritually Alive in the Chaos of the Modern World*. WaterBrook.

Chapter 13:

    1.   Tolkien, J. (2012d). *The Two Towers: Being the Second Part of The Lord of the Rings (The Lord of the Rings, 2)* (Reprint). William Morrow Paperbacks.

    2.   Tolkien, J. R. R. (1994). *The Lord of the Rings Part Three The Return of the King*. Ballantine / Del Rey.

Chapter 14:

    1.   Lewis, C. S. (1971). *The Magician's Nephew* (Later Printing). Collier Books.

    2.   Ortlund, D. C. (2020). *Gentle and Lowly: The Heart of Christ for Sinners and Sufferers*. Crossway Books.

    3.   Warren, T. H. (2021). *Prayer in the Night: For Those Who Work or Watch or Weep*. Amsterdam University Press.

Chapter 15:

1. Keller, T. (2014). *Every Good Endeavor: Connecting Your Work to God's Work* (Reprint). Penguin Books.

2. Warren, T. H. (2021). *Prayer in the Night: For Those Who Work or Watch or Weep*. Amsterdam University Press.

3. Martin Luther. (n.d.). AZQuotes.com. Retrieved December 31, 2022, from AZQuotes.com Web site: https://www.azquotes.com/quote/1394861.

4. Comer, J. M. (2017). *Garden City: Work, Rest, and the Art of Being Human.* (Reprint). Zondervan.

Chapter 16:

1. Capra, F. (Director). (1947b, January 7). *It's A Wonderful Life*. Liberty Films.

2. Warren, T. H. (2021). *Prayer in the Night: For Those Who Work or Watch or Weep*. Amsterdam University Press.

3. Lewis, C. S. (1960). Is Theology Poetry. *They Asked for a Paper (1962)*.

Made in the USA
Middletown, DE
31 August 2023